# ON THE EXISTENCE AND RELEVANCE OF GOD

# On the Existence and Relevance of God

Clement Dore

*Emeritus Professor of Philosophy*
*Vanderbilt University*

St. Martin's Press
New York

ON THE EXISTENCE AND RELEVANCE OF GOD
Copyright © 1996 by Clement Dore
All rights reserved. No part of this book may be used or reproduced
in any manner whatsoever without written permission except in the
case of brief quotations embodied in critical articles or reviews.
For information, address:

St. Martin's Press, Scholarly and Reference Division,
175 Fifth Avenue, New York, N.Y. 10010

First published in the United States of America in 1996

Printed in Great Britain

ISBN 0–312–12895–9

Library of Congress Cataloging-in-Publication Data
Dore, Clement, 1930–
On the existence and relevance of God / Clement Dore.
p.   cm.
Includes bibliographical references and index.
ISBN 0–312–12895–9
1. God.   2. God—Proof, Ontological.   3. Ethics.   4. Theism.
5. Phenomenalism.   I. Title.
BT102.D669   1996
212—dc20                                        95–39868
                                                    CIP

To the memory of

Roderick Firth

# Contents

# Preface

My main aims in this book are (1) to establish that it is rational to believe that God exists; (2) to show how God relates to morality; and (3) to show how God is causally connected to his creation.

With respect to (1), I defend a version of the ontological argument and refute the atheistic argument from suffering. In connection with (2), I argue that only God can account for the overridingness of morality. I also treat ethical supernaturalism as a type of ethical attitude theory, that is, I show how it is related to secular theories which base valid judgments of moral goodness and badness on pro and con attitudes. With respect to (3), I show precisely how, given scientific explanation, theistic explanation of the empirical universe can get a foothold. My method is to adopt and defend a version of theistic (Berkeley-like) phenomenalism and, in that connection, a pragmatic-instrumentalist interpretation of scientific theories.

All of the following have saved me from making some mistakes: Scott Davison, James Montmarquet, Crispin Sartwell and William Shaw. There might well be still fewer mistakes in the book as it stands, had I not sometimes not heeded their advice.

*Santa Cruz, California*                                   CLEMENT DORE

# 1

# The Concept of Supreme Perfection: Some Arguments for God's Existence

1.1 The following is a version of what, since Kant, has been called 'the ontological argument,' that is, an argument from the concept of a supremely perfect being to the *existence* of such a being:

(1) The concept of a supremely perfect being is, in part, the concept of a person who has all those properties which are such that it is better than not that a person jointly possesses them. Wisdom and power are examples. (I say 'jointly' because, for example, power without wisdom is not a perfection.)
(2) The concept of existence is the concept of such a property.
(3) So, it is a conceptual truth that a supremely perfect being possesses the property of existence.
(4) Hence, a supremely perfect being exists.

Since Kant, many philosophers have rejected arguments of this sort, on the ground that existence is not a property of persons. But it is also widely agreed that Frege was right in supposing that existence is a property of concepts, namely, the property of being instantiated. And my opening argument (call it 'OA₁') can be reformulated with that in view.

(1) The concept of a supremely perfect being is the concept of a being who has all supreme perfection-making properties.
(2) The concept of the concept of such a being being instantiated is the concept of a supreme perfection-making property (one that is necessary, though not sufficient, for supreme perfection).

(3)   So, it is a conceptual truth that the concept of a supremely perfect being is instantiated.

(4)   Hence, the concept of a supremely perfect being is instantiated, that is, a supremely perfect being exists.

However, for verbal economy (and doubts about the adequacy of the Fregean explication) I shall continue to say simply that the concept of existence *simpliciter* is the concept of a property which is such that it is better than not that a supremely perfect being possesses it.

1.2   Another objection to OA$_1$ is this – it is analogous to the following argument:

(a)   The concept of a square is in part the concept of a rectangle.

(b)   The concept of a rectangle is the concept of a figure which has more sides than three.

(c)   So, it is a conceptual truth that squares have more sides than three.

(d)   Hence, squares have more sides than three.

Now it is plain that step (c) does not entitle us to conclude that in fact there are squares. All that we can infer from it is the conditional proposition that *if* there are any squares, *then* they have more sides than three. And if that is not obvious enough, consider this argument:

(e)   The concept of a centaur is the concept of a being with the torso of a human being and the hindparts of a horse.

(f)   The concept of the hindparts of a horse is, in part, the concept of something which has a tail.

(g)   So, it is a conceptual truth that centaurs have tails.

(h)   Hence, centaurs have tails.

It is as clear as can be that all that step (g) warrants is the conditional proposition that *if* there are any centaurs, *then* they have tails. For surely steps (e) through (g) (all of which are true) do not entitle us to conclude that there are in fact centaurs.

But now, by parity of reasoning, all that steps (1) through (3) of OA$_1$ warrant us in concluding is that *if* a supremely perfect being exists, *then* a supremely perfect being exists. And this is a far cry from being able to conclude that there actually *is* a supremely perfect being.

The following is a reply to this objection: Sentences of the form 'S is P' express a conceptual truth if and only if the explanation of the fact that they express a truth lies entirely in the *concept* of S and the *concept* of P. Thus, the explanation of the fact that 'squares have more sides than three' expresses a conceptual truth lies entirely in the concept of a square and the concept of having more sides than three. But it is false that the explanation of the truth of 'If a supremely perfect being exists, then he exists' lies entirely in the concept of a supremely perfect being and the concept of existence. The concept of a supremely perfect being has no bearing whatever on the truth which is expressed by that sentence, since it would continue to express a true proposition, no matter what syntactically correct substitutions for 'supremely perfect being' we might make in it. The same does not hold true for the sentence 'If squares exist, then they have more sides than three'. That sentence would *not* continue to express a true proposition, no matter what syntactically correct substitutions for 'squares' we might make in it. And similar considerations apply to 'If centaurs exist, then they have tails'. (I shall have more to say about the nature of conceptual truths as we progress.)

But now (1) and (2) appear to have the same kind of epistemic bearing on (3) as do (a) and (b) on (c) and (e) and (f) on (g), that is, it looks as if (1) and (2) entail that it is in fact a conceptual truth that a supremely perfect being exists. However, as we have just seen, 'A supremely perfect being exists' does not express a conceptual truth if it means 'If a supremely perfect being exists, then he exists'. It looks, then, as if $OA_1$ really does establish the existence of God.

But here my critic may wish to continue as follows: 'All conceptual truths are analytic. Thus, it is a conceptual truth that centaurs have tails because 'centaur' means 'creature with the (normal) hindparts of a horse and the torso of a human being', and the former means in part 'creature with a tail'. And all analytic statements are reducible to ontologically insignificant conditionals. For let 'X-centaur' mean 'an existent centaur'. Then 'An X-centaur exists' is analytic. But unless it is equivalent to an ontologically insignificant conditional, namely, 'If an X-centaur exists, then it exists,' then a mere stipulative definition has existential significance.

'But now it must be the case that the reason that it is a conceptual truth that a supremely perfect being exists is that "supremely perfect being" means in part "a being which exists," so that "A supremely perfect being exists" is reducible to "A being which is supremely powerful, and so on, *and which exists*, exists." And this latter plainly has no more existential clout than does "An X-centaur (that is, an existent centaur) exists".'

However, this argument (call it 'the analyticity argument') can be seen to be a failure. For let 'X has actual existence' mean 'The sentence, "X exists" (1) expresses a truth and (2) is not equivalent in meaning to any ontologically insignificant conditional sentence.' Then we can advance the following argument (call it 'OA$_2$'):

(1)   The concept of a supremely perfect being is the concept of a being who has all supreme perfection-making properties.
(2)   The concept of having actual existence is the concept of a supreme perfection-making property.
(3)   So, it is a conceptual truth that a supremely perfect being has actual existence.
(4)   Hence, a supremely perfect being has actual existence, that is, the sentence 'A supremely perfect being exists' expresses an ontologically significant proposition.

Now suppose that my critic maintains, as against OA$_2$, that since it is indeed, a conceptual truth that a supremely perfect being has actual existence, it must be true that 'supremely perfect being' means, in part, 'being which has actual existence,' so that 'A supremely perfect being has actual existence' means 'A being who is supremely powerful, and so on, and *who has actual existence*, has actual existence'. It is clear that the latter sentence is strongly analogous to 'X-centaurs (existent centaurs) exist', so that if all that OA$_2$ warrants is the envisaged conclusion, then it is ontologically defunct.

But now consider the following definition. Let 'X has real, actual existence' mean ' "X has actual existence" (1) expresses a truth and (2) is not equivalent in meaning to any ontologically insignificant conditional sentence.' Then we can set out the following argument (call it 'OA$_3$'):

(1)   The concept of a supremely perfect being is the concept of a being who has every supreme perfection-making property.
(2)   The concept of having real, actual existence is the concept of a supreme perfection-making property.

(3)  So, it is a conceptual truth that a supremely perfect being has real, actual existence.

(4)  So, a supremely perfect being has real, actual existence, that is, 'a supremely perfect being has actual existence' expresses an ontologically significant proposition, that is, the conclusion of $OA_1$ is ontologically significant.

Now if my critic maintained at this point that 'supremely perfect being' means 'being who is supremely powerful, and so on, *and who has real, actual existence*,' so that all that $OA_3$ entitles us to conclude is the ontologically insignificant proposition that a being who has real, actual existence has real, actual existence (that is, that if such a being exists, then he has real, actual existence), then I would reply by introducing the concept of actual, real, actual existence; and, as we progressed, it would become more and more incredible that 'supremely perfect being' has such a grotesquely bloated meaning. (This is not a double-edged sword. Indeed, my meta-proofs are intended to show that the conclusions of the immediately preceding proofs are not analytic, but, rather, synthetic, conceptual truths.)

But is it the case that, say, 'A supremely perfect being has real, actual existence' differs in meaning from, say, 'A supremely perfect being has actual existence'? If not, then my rebuttal is a failure. But the answer is that they do differ in meaning, inasmuch as they refer to different sentence types and tokens. 'A supremely perfect being has actual existence' ascribes the property of ontological significance to the sentence (type and token), 'A supremely perfect being exists,' whereas 'A supremely perfect being has real, actual existence' ascribes ontological significance to a *different* sentence (type and token), namely, 'A supremely perfect being has actual existence'. And so on for 'A supremely perfect being has actual, real, actual existence' and so on.

Needless to say, I am not committing myself to the conclusion that different sentences cannot have the same meaning. Thus, I think that, say, 'This is a square' and 'This is an equilateral rectangle' mean the same, even though they are two different sentences. However, 'The sentence, "This is a square," is written on the blackboard' differs in meaning from 'The sentence, "This is an equilateral rectangle," is written on the blackboard', since here we are *mentioning* rather than *using* the sentences, 'This is a square' and 'This is an equilateral rectangle'. And if that is not clear enough, consider 'The sentence, "This is a square," contains four words' and

'The sentence, "This is an equilateral rectangle," contains four words'. They surely do not have the same meaning, since the former sentence expresses a truth and the latter sentence expresses a falsehood.

It should be stressed that we are not confronted by an unacceptable regress here, since once my critic grows weary, there are no further sentence tokens to enter into the regress; and surely sentence types do not exist in the absence of corresponding sentence tokens.

It follows that a supremely perfect being was only potentially a being who has, say, real, actual existence until my saying 'The sentence, "A supremely perfect being has actual existence" is ontologically significant' actualized that potentiality. And Aristotle and Aquinas held that unactualized potentiality is a mark of imperfection. But consider 'God would have loved Hitler more had Hitler been less vicious'. There are two things to be said about this sentence: (1) It shows that theists cannot avoid ascribing unactualized potentialities to God just by dispensing with $OA_1$-type arguments, and, more importantly, (2) it is surely not a defect in God that he would have loved Hitler more had Hitler been less vicious.

But is it not the case that there are no *other* instances of conceptual truths which are not clearly essentially conditional truths? And does that not render my arguments suspect? The answer to the former question is 'No'. For it is far from clear that, say, 'It is a conceptual truth that the whole number between the number eight and the number ten is odd' means the same as 'It is a conceptual truth that if there is a whole number between the number eight and the number ten, then it is odd' or 'If the number eight and the number ten exist and there is a whole number between them, then it is odd'. And such examples can, of course, be multiplied indefinitely.

1.3    Another reply to my critic is now available. Not only must he reject $OA_1$, but an indefinitely large number of meta-proofs, until he grows weary. He, on the other hand, has only one argument on behalf of his position, namely, the argument that there are no other instances of nonconditional conceptual truths. And, as we have just seen, that is far from clearly cogent.

Here my critic may wish to argue that, nonetheless, it has some cogency, and, since it refutes $OA_1$, it *ipso facto* refutes all of the envisaged meta-proofs; so that my multiplying the latter results in no epistemic gain. But, as every philosopher knows, one person's *modus ponens* is another person's *modus tollens*. And I submit that it is incredible that the envisaged argument refutes *all* of the meta-proofs, and, hence, that it is incredible that it refutes $OA_1$.

1.4  But don't my arguments establish, not just the existence of one supremely perfect being, but the existence of an indefinitely large number of supremely perfect beings? And isn't that a good reason to suppose that something is wrong with them? The answer is that since the concept of a supremely perfect being is, among other things, the concept of a being who is the uncreated creator of everything else, it is a conceptual (necessary) truth that any supremely perfect being there may be is the uncreated creator of everything else, and, hence, positing two or more supremely perfect beings commits one to the logically absurd conclusion that there are beings who are both created and uncreated.

Let me elaborate. Let us individuate the envisaged supremely perfect beings by naming them. Call one of them '$God_1$', another '$God_2$', and yet another '$God_3$', and so on. And suppose that $God_1$ is necessarily an uncreated creator of everything else. Then $God_2$ and $God_3$, and so on, are both created (by $God_1$) and yet, *qua* supremely perfect beings, uncreated by anyone else. Hence, they are logically impossible. And what is logically impossible is surely not something with respect to which existence is a perfection, that is, the concept of a logically impossible state of affairs is not such that the concept of its obtaining is the concept of a perfection relative to that state of affairs. Logically impossible states of affairs are such that it is better than not that they do not obtain. The reason is this: A necessarily false proposition entails every proposition. So if a logically impossible state of affairs obtained, then the world would be intolerably chaotic.

It is, of course, true that since 'A logically impossible state of affairs obtains' is itself a necessary falsehood, it entails as well that the world would *not* be intolerably chaotic. But, since it *would* be intolerably chaotic nonetheless, it is clearly better than not that no logically impossible state of affairs obtains, that is, other things being equal, a world which is not intolerably chaotic *simpliciter* is better than a world which is both *not* intolerably chaotic *and* intolerably chaotic, or, at any rate, other things being equal, a world, *in which only one supremely perfect being exists*, and is not intolerably chaotic *simpliciter* is better than a world, in which there is *more* than one supremely perfect being, and which is both not intolerably chaotic and intolerably chaotic.

But now what about *nearly* supremely perfect beings – beings who have all of the perfections of a supremely perfect being *except* being the uncreated creator of everything else? The answer is that the concept of a supremely perfect being is also the concept of a being who cannot possibly be surpassed *or even rivaled* with respect to the number and degree of his perfections, and, hence, that nearly supremely perfect beings are also logically impossible, so that it is not better than not that they exist.

But suppose that someone introduces the concept of *minor deities*, that is, beings who possess *some* properties which are perfections relative to a supremely perfect being, including existence, but far fewer and to a far less degree. How are we to deal with this concept? The answer is that, on this definition, 'Minor deities exist' means, in part, 'Existent beings, who possess some of a supremely perfect being's perfections, exist'; and that sentence would continue to express a truth under any syntactically correct substitutions for 'beings who possess some of a supremely perfect being's perfections'. But vacuous truths of this sort are subject to translation into vacuous, ontologically sterile conditionals. Otherwise, sentences such as 'Existent centaurs (dragons, and so on) exist' would commit us to a distressingly bloated ontology. It follows that 'Minor deities exist' is equivalent in meaning to the ontologically sterile conditional sentence, 'If minor deities exist, then they exist'. 'Minor deities [thus defined] exist' is demonstrably and, indeed, intuitively, ontologically sterile.

It would also be unacceptable to define 'minor deities' as 'beings who possess all properties (whatever they may be) which are perfections relative to a supremely perfect being, except . . .' where 'existence' is not a fill-in. For the concept of supreme perfection is such that the number of perfections which would be able to fill in is a mere drop in the ocean with respect to the totality of the perfections of a supremely perfect being: it is physically impossible for us to fill in enough exceptions to render minor deities, defined in the envisaged manner, logically possible. This is because the number of perfections, which we could fill in, constitutes just a small percentage of the perfections of a supremely perfect being, and, hence, any possible world, in which a supremely perfect being and a minor deity existed, would be a world in which the latter possessed a *high percentage* of the perfections of a supremely perfect being. And there is no such possible world. But since, as we have seen, it is a conceptual truth that a supremely perfect being exists, and, hence, a supremely perfect being exists in every possible world, there is no possible world in which a minor deity exists. Minor deities, like nearly supremely perfect beings, are logically impossible, and so it is not better than not that they exist.

I am arguing in effect that if the contemplated versions of the ontological argument are sound, then the concepts of nearly supremely perfect beings and minor deities are logically incoherent, and hence, that it is not better than not that they exist. But my opponent is claiming that if $OA_1$, and so on, are sound, then the parodies are sound as well. And we can both be right only if $OA_1$, and so on, are not sound. So my opponent is begging the question.

But isn't the analysis of the concept of supreme perfection, which I adduce vis-a-vis the parodies, *ad hoc*? I submit that it is sufficiently intuitive so that there is no plausible rival explanation of what is wrong with the contemplated parodies. Moreover, there is a simple argument that my analysis is not *ad hoc*: It is certainly a correct analysis of the concept of *God*. It is, for example, plainly a conceptual truth that if God exists, then he is the uncreated creator of everything else. But the concept of God is the concept of a supremely perfect being. And it follows from the fact that the concept of God is the concept of an uncreated creator *and* the concept of a supremely perfect being that it is a conceptual truth that God is both a supremely perfect being and an uncreated creator. And it follows in turn that it is a conceptual truth that there is an individual who is both an uncreated creator and a supremely perfect being, that is, it is a conceptual truth that there is only one supremely perfect being. Similar considerations apply to the fact that the concept of God is both the concept of a supremely perfect being and the concept of a being who cannot be surpassed or even rivaled with respect to the number and degree of his perfections. (I have formulated $OA_1$, and so on, in terms of the concept of a supremely perfect being, since I think that those arguments would be less perspicuous were we to substitute 'God' for 'supremely perfect being'.)

1.5 I have said that no one can rival God with respect to the number and degree of his perfections. But someone may argue that *existence* is a property which does not vary in degree, which is possessed by all of us, and, hence, *is* a perfection with respect to which we rival God (given that God exists).

But the claim that in fact there are degrees of existence can be made plausible by the consideration that, for example, 'Jones, the sculptor, has partially completed a statue,' does not, since it is an entirely unexceptional locution, predicate 'partially completed' of a nonexistent object, and so is plainly logically incompatible with 'It is false that there is a statue which Jones has partially completed'. The former sentence affirms that the completed statue exists but not fully and, hence, that what Jones has brought about, which *does* fully exist, is identical with, but not fully identical with, the completed statue.

I have said that 'Jones, the sculpture, has partially completed a statue' does not predicate 'partially completed' of a nonexistent object. And someone may object that it does not follow that it predicates 'partially completed' of the completed, though only partially existent, statue, but rather that it predicates 'partially completed' of the partially completed statue. But this will not do. For if 'Jones, the sculptor, has partially completed a statue' were best explicated by 'Jones has partially completed a partially completed statue,' then the latter sentence would expand into 'Jones has partially completed a statue which is partially partially completed,' and so on *ad infinitum*. And, anyway, the claim that the contemplated explication captures the meaning of the original sentence (call it S) is obviously absurd.

A better objection is that S does not predicate 'partially completed' of anything, existent or nonexistent, but rather simply affirms that Jones has produced a certain object – namely, a partially completed statue. My reply is that a partially completed statue is a statue which is partially completed, that is, that 'Jones has produced a partially completed statue' itself predicates 'partially completed' of a statue. Reasonable people could, no doubt, disagree about this explication, were it not for the fact that we appear to have an argument for the existence of a being who cannot be rivaled with respect to any of his perfections, including his existence.

Similar considerations hold with respect to self-identity. It is better than not that God is identical with himself rather than some other being, just because it is better than not that he *exists*. And, once again, it is plausible that there are degrees of existence.

It follows from the unrivalability of God that human beings do not attain a degree of consciousness which rivals the degree of consciousness which God enjoys. But there are, we are told by users of psychedelic drugs, degrees of consciousness which normal human beings never attain. And it is not implausible to suppose then that the degree of consciousness which those drug-takers achieve is vastly surpassed by *God's* degree of consciousness.

Finally, it also follows that there are degrees of being justified in holding a given belief, which human beings never attain. Again, this claim is in need of defense. But I submit that my argument for the existence of a supremely perfect being is just such a defense. This does not entail that there are no self-evident propositions relative to human beings – only that there are degrees of self-evidence.

Here someone may object as follows: 'Since it is a conceptual truth that God exists, it is a *necessary* truth that God exists, that is, God exists necessarily. But it looks as if, say *numbers* rival God with respect to *that* perfection.' The answer is that if numbers exist necessarily, their necessary existence, unlike God's, is derivative, that is, God, the necessarily existent, uncreated creator of everything else, *necessarily* creates numbers. And nonderivative necessity is a greater perfection than derivative necessity.

1.6   Here it may be said that, though it may be impossible to surpass, or even rival, God with respect to the *total amount* of power which he possesses, it is possible to surpass God with respect to at least one *specific* power, namely, the power to destroy oneself. Or, at any rate, it may be said that I am committed to that conclusion by my claim that it is a conceptual truth and, hence, a *necessary* truth, that God exists. For if God exists necessarily, then God cannot destroy himself.

But as I said at the outset of this chapter, power *per se* is not a perfection. It is a perfection only when it is conjoined with wisdom – and, let me add, goodness. But God's destroying himself would be incompatible with his goodness. Hence, it may look as if he had the ability to destroy himself, then this would be a defect rather than a perfection. And it appears to follow that, though some of us have the power to destroy ourselves and God does not, it is false that we can surpass God with respect to any *perfection* of his.

But why would God's being able to destroy himself be a defect if in fact he never exercised that ability? The answer is that since it is a conceptual truth that God, a supremely perfect being, exists, it is a necessary truth that he exists *qua* supremely perfect being and, hence, it is a necessary truth that he does not engage in wrongdoing, from which it follows that he has no capacity for wrongdoing. Suppose, then, that *per impossible* God was able to do wrong. Then, he would *not* exist necessarily and since, if he exists, he exists necessarily, he would not exist *simpliciter*. Hence, though a capacity for wrongdoing would not, strictly speaking, be a *defect* in God, it is nonetheless true that, since it is logically incompatible with his very existence, it would certainly not be a *perfection* in him.

1.7   The foregoing should make the ontological arguer more comfortable about the Gaunilo-strategy.[1] If in fact the one and only supremely perfect being has some kind of body (for example, the body of Gaunilo's perfect island), at least it is demonstrable that there is only *one* of him. Moreover, it can be shown that a supremely perfect being would be essentially disembodied.

Physical objects have the following two characteristics: (1) It is logically impossible for them to have a nonspatial existence. (2) They are such that, for any set of spatial locations at a given moment, M, it is possible that they do not occupy any of those spatial locations at M. Suppose for simplicity, that there are just two spatial locations, $PL_1$ and $PL_2$, and just one physical object O. Then it is possible that O occupies neither $PL_1$ nor $PL_2$ at M. But *ex hypothesi* these are the only spatial locations that there are. Moreover, *ex hypothesi* it is a necessary truth that if O exists, then it exists at some spatial location or other. It follows that it is possible that O does not exist *simpliciter* at M. But this would be false if O were a necessarily existent individual. Hence, any such individual is essentially nonspatial, that is, essentially disembodied. It follows that the one and only supremely perfect being is, since he exists necessarily, essentially disembodied. And this entails in turn that he is not essentially a perfect island or centaur or unicorn, and so on.

There is another argument that God is essentially disembodied. Able-bodied human beings frequently can prevent themselves from being at a given spatial location, P, at a given moment, M. Moreover, there is no good reason to think that God's having that power – and to a far greater extent than we do – would be incompatible with his goodness and/or wisdom, that is, there is no good reason to think that God's having that power would not be a perfection in God. So, even if it is in fact false that any physical object is such that there is no spatial location with respect to which it is not possible that it does not occupy it, it is nonetheless demonstrable that this is true of God. But if every place is such that it is possible that God does not occupy it, then either it is possible that God does not exist, or it is possible that he does not exist in space. But God exists necessarily, and, hence, it is not possible that he does not exist. But, once again, physical objects are *not* such that it is possible that they do not exist in space. So God is not a physical object.

1.8   Another Gaunilo-type criticism goes as follows: 'Consider the concept of a supremely *imperfect* being – a being who possesses all those properties which are such that it is worse than not that he jointly possesses them. The concept of existence is among those properties. So it is a conceptual truth that a supremely imperfect being exists.

'Now a supremely imperfect being, like a supremely perfect being, would be necessarily preeminently powerful, that is, no other individual could possibly surpass, or even rival, him, with respect to his power. So if a supremely imperfect being exists, then the existence of a supremely perfect being is not logically possible. And, of course, *vice versa*.

'It follows that there is something wrong with at least one of the envisaged pair of arguments. But it is surely unlikely that there is a defect in one of those arguments, which is such that the other one does not suffer from an analogous defect.'

So goes the criticism: It can be met, I think, in the following manner: A supremely imperfect being would either recognize that he is morally imperfect or he would not. But a person's recognition of his own moral imperfection is, normally at least, a virtue (a perfection) rather than a vice (an imperfection). Moreover, a person's *not* recognizing that he is morally imperfect makes him *less* morally culpable than he would otherwise be, so it, too, is a perfection rather than an imperfection.

It may be objected here that a person's failure to recognize his imperfections is a good thing only if it is not the result of culpable ignorance. But I submit that a person's being culpably ignorant about his imperfections amounts to his in fact *recognizing* those imperfections but willingly concealing that recognition from himself. And a supremely knowledgeable being would not be capable of such self-deception. For if he were, then he would be rivaled and, indeed, surpassed by some human beings with respect to his knowledge: he would not after all be supremely knowledge-able, and, hence, would not after all have all those properties which are such that it is better than not that they not be jointly possessed.

Here it may be said that a person's recognition of his own imperfection is a perfection only in those who, on the basis of that recognition, will try to reform. But I submit that it is sufficiently plausible that the world would have been a better place had Hitler explicitly recognized how morally monstrous he was just before he died than if he did not, so that it is plausible that (a) the concept of a supremely imperfect being is logically incoherent and (b) we have no analogous reason for thinking that the concept of a supremely perfect being is logically incoherent.

But isn't it the case that only if a person's explicit recognition of his moral monstrousness *is accompanied by self-loathing*, that it is better, rather than worse, that he has that recognition? The answer is that it is a *conceptual* truth that anyone who explicitly recognizes his gross moral imperfections regrets that he has them: 'I know that I am a morally monstrous person, but I am perfectly contented with that' surely has the ring of absurdity.

But isn't it implausible on its face that a person's recognizing his gross moral imperfections, *and* his *not* recognizing them, are both perfections? The answer is that from a utilitarian point of view, it is frequently much better than not that a person recognizes his moral imperfections, since this may cause him to reform. But a person may recognize his moral imperfections and (due, say, to weakness of will) fail to reform. And *that* kind of person would be better off, because less morally culpable, if he did *not* have the envisaged self-knowledge.

Now it is a necessary truth that a supremely imperfect person would *not* reform as a result of recognition-cum-remorse, with respect to his moral imperfections. So, though his recognition-cum-remorse would be a good thing, his not having that recognition-cum-remorse would also be a good thing, since, in that event, he would not be as morally culpable. It follows, once again, that the concept of a supremely imperfect being is logically incoherent. And we lack an analogous argument for the claim that this is true as well of the concept of a supremely perfect being.

1.9   If the arguments of the preceding sections are right, then 'God exists' is intuitively an ontologically significant conceptual truth. If those arguments are sound, then it is intuitive that God exists necessarily. But if a proposition, p, is, if true, necessarily true, then p is, if false, necessarily false. For suppose that there is a possible world in which p is true. Then in that world it is necessarily true.

And what is necessarily true in one possible world (for example, '7 + 5 = 12') is necessarily true in the actual one. (There is no possible world in which what is a contingent proposition in the actual world, for example, 'Grass is green,' is necessarily true.) It follows that if p is false, then it is not (even) possibly true.

So we can construct an additional argument for God's existence:

(1)   If God is not logically impossible, then God exists necessarily.
(2)   God is not logically impossible.
(3)   Hence, God exists necessarily.

Of course, this argument does not constitute an epistemic gain unless (2) is subject to defense. But in fact a defense is available:

(a)   The concept of a supremely perfect being is the concept of a being which has all supreme perfection-making properties.
(b)   The concept of the concept of such a being *being logically coherent* is the concept of a supreme perfection-making property.
(c)   So, it is a conceptual truth that the concept of a supremely perfect being is logically coherent.
(d)   Hence, the concept of a supremely perfect being is in fact logically coherent.

Once again, someone may claim at this point that all that (c) actually warrants is the ontologically insignificant conclusion that *if* the concept of a supremely perfect being is instantiated, *then* that concept is logically coherent. But meta-proofs, which are analogous to the meta-proofs of 1.2 and 1.3, are available at this point. Thus 'The concept of X is *actually* logically coherent' means 'The sentence "The concept of X is logically coherent" (1) expresses a truth and (2) is not reducible to an ontologically insignificant conclusion.' Then we can get a meta-proof of the envisaged sort simply by noting that the concept of its concept being *actually* logically coherent is the concept of a supreme perfection-making property. And until my critic grows weary, I can fall back on *real*, actual logical coherence; and so on indefinitely.

1.10   But can't we establish, by analogous arguments, the logical possibility of nearly supremely perfect beings and of minor deities? The answer is 'No'. If we were to accept the proposition that nearly supremely perfect beings and minor deities are logically possible, then we would be committed to the ontologically disastrous conclusion that what is (demonstrably) impossible (see 1.4) is (also) possible. So we have a very good reason for rejecting the claim that it is better than not that the concepts of nearly supremely perfect beings and minor deities be logically coherent. A simpler reply is just that if those concepts were logically coherent, then nearly supremely perfect beings and minor deities would exist. And this would diminish the solitary splendor of the supremely perfect being. Hence, once again, it is not better than not that their concepts are logically coherent; and so the envisaged possibility parodies collapse.

1.11    I have argued for the existence of an uncreated creator of everything else. But now the question arises as to precisely how he relates to his creation. In Chapter 7, I shall argue in effect that the theist can, and should, adopt a theory of the nature of God's creativity which is (a) independent of any scientific theory and (b) reflects the traditional belief that God's causation is contemporaneous. First, however, I want to show that the traditional atheistic argument from suffering does not overthrow what is surely at least a *prima facie* case on behalf of my arguments being sound.

The nature of the debate, between the ontological arguer and the atheist, which I have in mind, is this: The atheist claims (a) that widespread suffering is strong evidence against the existence of God, and *a fortiori* that it is evidence that there is *something* wrong with the arguments of this chapter, whether or not the atheist can tell us exactly *what* is wrong, and (b) that the ontological arguer needs to show that in fact it is the argument from suffering, and not the arguments of this chapter, which is defective.

It is, of course, open to the ontological arguer to employ a *tu quoque* argument here, that is, to maintain that the arguments of this chapter show that there is *something* wrong with the argument from suffering, regardless of whether the ontological arguer can specify the *nature* of its defectiveness.

But the ontological arguer, who uses that move as his only defense, is in effect admitting that he and the atheistic arguer from suffering have arrived at a hopeless impasse. In 3.1–3.4 I shall argue that the ontological arguer can do much better, that is, that he can show precisely *why* the argument from suffering is noncogent and, hence, does not undermine the arguments of this chapter.

# 2

# The Argument from Suffering I

2.1 The atheistic argument from suffering can be put very succinctly. 'If there is a supremely powerful and knowledgeable person, then he can abolish the widespread suffering that we find in the world. (Even you and I can abolish *some* of it.) But if he were supremely good, then he *would* abolish it (or, at least, diminish it). Hence, there is no being who is supremely powerful, supremely knowledgeable and supremely good, that is, a supremely perfect being does not exist.'

2.2 An early version of Alvin Plantinga's free will defense against this argument[1] can be formulated as follows: 'It is a perfection in God that he has created other persons. And it is better that these persons be free moral agents, rather than innocent automata. But since freely doing what is right requires an ability to do otherwise, free moral agents must have a capacity for wrongdoing. Moreover, it is logically impossible[2] for God to *cause* someone to refrain from wrongdoing while allowing him to do so freely. Hence, even though he is supremely powerful, it is not in God's power to prevent the harm which is done by free moral wrongdoers, so long as he permits free moral agency. And since the positive value of free right choices outweighs the negative value of harmful, wrong choices, and, since we free moral agents frequently freely choose to do what is right, God is justified in permitting the harm which we do.'

An objection to this defense is that, since there is an indefinitely large number of sets of individuating person-properties, it must be that the instantiation of *some* of those sets would, though they had a capacity for wrongdoing, never exercise it. But Plantinga replies that it may be that it is a brute (and unhappy) fact that every set of individuating person-properties which contains the property, 'free with respect to morally significant actions,' will, if instantiated, sometimes freely do what is morally wrong.[3]

But isn't this claim highly implausible in view of the indefinitely large number of such sets which God had to choose from? J. L. Mackie writes as follows about this:

> How is it possible that every [such set is thus afflicted?] This possibility would be realized only if God were faced with a limited range of creaturely essences, a limited number of possible people from which he had to make a selection, if he was to create free agents at all. What can be supposed to have presented him with that limited range?[4]

What Mackie says here is not so much a reasoned refutation of Plantinga as, rather, a claim that the free will defense is, on its face, implausible.


2.3   The following is a response to Mackie's criticism: 'Suppose that God were disposed to fail to instantiate any set of individuating person-properties (any person-essence), which contained the property, "free with respect to morally significant actions" (call such an essence "an E-essence"), were that essence such that, if instantiated, it would sometimes do what is morally wrong. And consider a given instantiated essence, Jones, whom God would not have instantiated, had he been going to engage in wrongdoing. Could Jones be an instantiated E-essence? The answer is "No" for the following reason: It follows from the fact that God possesses the envisaged disposition with respect to Jones that if Jones had been going to perform a morally wrong action on a given occasion, O, barring God's exercising that disposition, then Jones would not have existed – or, at any rate, he would not have existed on that occasion. And it is plainly false that a person can be able to do something on a given occasion when, had he been going to do it, then he would not have existed then: a person's existing is a necessary condition of that person's performing any action and *a fortiori* it is a necessary condition of a person's *having it in his power* to perform any action. It follows that "Jones had it in his power to do wrong on O, though if he had been going to do wrong on O, he would not have existed then" is no more acceptable than, say, "Jones had it in his power to swim on O, even, though, if he had been going to swim on O, there would have been no liquid in his vicinity then".'

'The foregoing does not entail that God could not have instantiated person-essences which would in fact, if instantiated, have freely performed actions of refraining from wrongdoing and would never have performed any wrong actions. Hence, Mackie's criticism of Plantinga does not apply here. But, given that a world in which God's creatures frequently freely avoid wrongdoing is better than any world in which there is no free avoidance of wrongdoing, the foregoing does show that God would have been morally justified in *not* being disposed to prevent the wrongdoing of perfect-person-instantiations if (contrary to fact) he foresaw that they would sometimes do wrong.[5] And that is enough to support the claim that God is not reprehensible for permitting the wrongdoing of the instantiations of the person-essences whom he in fact instantiates. For there is no morally relevant difference between God's being disposed to permit (what is contrary to fact) wrongdoing on the part of perfect-person-instantiations and his being disposed to permit the wrongdoing in which his non-perfect creatures in fact engage.'

2.4   According to the paradigm case argument for the compatibility of being able to do otherwise with big-bang determinism, we are able to recognize paradigm cases of being able to do otherwise, regardless of whether big-bang determinism is true or false. Thus, it is claimed that we know that I married someone of my own free will, if we know that I was not coerced into marrying her either by an irate parent or by a hypnotist or by a drug and that I did not marry her freely if I was thus coerced. And it is also maintained that we know that the question whether big-bang determinism is true has no bearing on this kind of mundane example. Moreover, it is further claimed that similar considerations apply to what we may call 'theological determinism' – the thesis that *God* is the ultimate cause of our choices and actions. And the conclusion is that God's bringing it about that only perfect people exist is compatible with free moral agency.

But now suppose that I learned that all of my choices until now, no matter how mundane, had been produced by a hypnotist. Would I, under those circumstances, be justified in concluding that what I took to be paradigm cases of free choice really were occasions on which I chose freely?

Here the paradigm case arguer may say, 'We are highly justified in believing that at least most of our choices are *not* the result of hypnosis. And it follows that we are highly justified in believing that what appear to be paradigm cases of free choice really are such paradigm cases'. But once the paradigm case arguer admits that what appear to be paradigm cases of free choice are *possibly* not such cases, he cannot rebut the claim that rational and intelligent people, who reflected on the question of whether determinism is true, would conclude that what appear to be paradigm cases of being able to do otherwise are not in reality that, if in fact determinism is true.

A simple argument that rational and intelligent people would arrive at that conclusion is as follows: I choose and act freely only if my choices and actions are not brought about by causes over which I have no control. Thus, if a choice of mine *in present time* has a certain sufficient causal condition, the existence or operation of which I am powerless to prevent (say, my being drugged or hypnotized against my will), then it is not a free choice. But if big-bang determinism (on the macroscopic level) is correct, then any choice and action of mine is the end product of a causal series which stretches back to the big bang, that is, to *a time long before I was born* and *a fortiori* to a time when I had no control over events which would turn out to be causally sufficient for those choices and actions. Plainly, it will not do to say that, though I may well regret having been drugged or hypnotized, I do not regret events that occurred long before I was born, and that this consideration shows that the concept of free choice is such that big-bang determinism is in fact compatible with it. For if I am a reflective big-bang determinist, who has done something which I deeply regret, I may well come to regret as well the fact that the past before I was born was precisely as it was. It follows that free will is incompatible with big-bang determinism, and so anyone who claims that it is compatible with theological determinism owes us an explanation of why that should be so. And I know of no philosopher who has attempted to formulate such an explanation.

2.5   If the free will defender is to apply his solution to the problem of moral evil to suffering which is not the result of the vicious choices of human moral agents (suffering due to unpreventable diseases and natural calamities, such as earthquakes), then he must attribute this suffering to the vicious choices of nonearthly moral agents. And it may be thought that this move is totally unacceptable.

But from a dialectical point of view, the envisaged move is understandable, given what many theists take to be the epistemic status of belief in God. For many theists believe that, even though there is no evidence for God's existence, there is no evidence against it; and this entails that they believe that the claim that God is the ultimate cause of the empirical universe is such that there is no evidence against it. And it seems reasonable to suppose that, given that there is no evidence against *that* claim, then there is also no evidence against the thesis that nonearthly moral agents are ultimately responsible for some of the world's woes.[6] The opponent of the present version of the free will defense may want to say here that it is not enough to have no evidence against a given belief. Rather, it is rational for one to hold it only if it is self-evident or there is external evidence for it. But this is controversial, as is shown by Plantinga's defense of what he calls 'nonevidentialism'[7] and also by Gilbert Harman's negative coherentism, that is, the thesis that any belief is *prima facie* justified in the sense that it is rational to hold it unless there is evidence against it.[8] And the free will defender's critic would obviously be begging the question were he to maintain at this point that, since no rebuttal of the atheistic argument from suffering, including the free will defense, is successful, there is in fact evidence against the thesis that God exists and *a fortiori* against the claim that God, the ultimate cause of the empirical universe, exists.

2.6   Harry G. Frankfurt has presented a criticism of the thesis that being morally responsible for doing something, X, entails being able to do other than X.[9] And it may be thought that this criticism undermines the contemplated reply to Mackie. The criticism goes roughly as follows: 'Suppose that someone, Smith, has it in his power to see to it that another person, Jones, does something, X, which Smith wants him to do, and is disposed to cause Jones to do it if Jones will not do it on his own. And suppose further that Black would prefer that Jones himself decides to do, and does, X. Then if, in fact, Jones himself brings it about that he does X, he is morally responsible for doing it, even though, because of the envisaged disposition of Smith, he could not have done otherwise. The reason is that Jones did not do it *because* he could not have done otherwise. Rather Jones *would* have done it even if he *could* have done otherwise, that is, even if Black had *not* been going to prevent him from not doing it. And it follows that Jones is morally responsible for having done it.'

Now the Jones whom I have discussed in my reply to Mackie might well be in a position similar to Frankfurt's Jones. For it might well be that, though, *ex hypothesi*, Jones could not do other than perform a morally right action on any given occasion, when in fact he performs one, he would have performed those actions even if he had been able to do otherwise. And if this latter were true, then Jones' actions would be morally praiseworthy, even though in fact he would not be able to do other than perform them. And surely morally praiseworthy actions are all that the free will defender could justifiably desire, regardless of whether the person who performs them is able to do otherwise.

One response to this criticism is that it is false that there are a myriad of person-essences who would, if instantiated, always do what is right 'on their own,' that is, without being prevented by God from doing what is wrong. However, given this reply, Mackie-like doubts re-emerge.

There is another response: 'A world in which moral agents are in fact able to do other than what is right is a world in which their moral obligations are vastly more stringent than they would be in the envisaged Frankfurt-like world, even given (what is doubtful) that there could be any moral obligations at all in such a world. And the free fulfilling of truly stringent obligations is more intrinsically valuable than is the fulfilling of obligations which have no stringency (if such there be). The essential idea here is this: the greater the failure which would have resulted, in the event that a moral agent had violated a moral obligation, the more splendid (intrinsically valuable) is her not violating it. And that accounts for its being the case that the actual world contains more intrinsic value than does the contemplated Frankfurt-like world.

However, this reply can be doubted. I submit that most of us are so strongly disinclined to rape children that that disinclination amounts of a compulsion, that is, we are not (psychologically) able to do it, and therefore we cannot freely refrain from doing it. Now suppose that a person is not thus compelled to refrain from raping children but freely chooses not to. It is surely controversial that the world is a better place because of that state of affairs. For *not* being compelled not to rape children may well appear to be a character defect: it may well appear that a person who has to resist the temptation to rape children is, to that extent, defective, even if he always succeeds.

It will not do for the free will defender to maintain here that a human person's being tempted to rape children may be the result of the evil choices of non-human moral agents. For that raises the question of whether it is really a good thing that *those* moral agents have *that* option.

Here it may be said that God's permitting some people to be tempted to rape children *and* to succumb to that temptation is a (logically) necessary condition of a human person's being able freely to respond to the suffering of the victims. But we have no moral obligation to perform acts of supererogation; and, so far as a person's having a moral obligation to relieve suffering *when he can easily do so*, it is, once again, true that a person has that obligation only if he can do otherwise, that is, only if he has some *contrary* inclination. But it looks as if *that* inclination *also* constitutes a character defect in a person, even if he never acts on it. And, anyway, the envisaged rebuttal does not really come to grips with the contention that the world is worse, rather than better, because there are people who are tempted to rape children, even though some of them never succumb to that temptation.

Or, at any rate, that is sufficiently plausible so that, at a minimum, reasonable people can disagree. Let us turn, then, to other attempts to rebut the argument from suffering. I shall return to a discussion of the free will defense in 3.7, 3.8 and 3.9.

2.7 It is plausible that a person is not justified in failing to prevent intense and prolonged suffering, which he can easily prevent, unless his doing so is necessary for preventing still further suffering. Call this thesis 'T'. If T is true and God is justified in causing suffering, then much of our suffering must be such that if we had not suffered to *that* extent, then we would have suffered still more.

But it sometimes surely happens that a person's suffering while dying is the result of an injury which caused her to experience *more* suffering in the past than she would have, if it were not for that injury. Now suppose that she had not suffered on her deathbed. Then she would have suffered *less*, not more, in the past; and, hence, it is false that the total amount of suffering which she undergoes in this life, at least, is such that if she had not suffered to *that* extent, then she would have suffered to an even *greater* extent. It follows that either the defender of the present solution of the problem of suffering (call it 'Ø') must posit an afterlife in which the contemplated sufferer would have suffered more if it were not for her earthly suffering, or he must maintain that many *other* sentient beings would have suffered more in this life than in fact they did, were it not for her earthly suffering. The latter claim may appear to be only a dubious justification of the ways of God to man, since it may look as if it entails that God is an unfair utilitarian. (I shall discuss it again in 4.7.) But how plausible is the former claim? I think that, for a reason which will emerge in 3.12, it is as plausible as the envisaged alternative. Or, at any rate, this is true if the contemplated sufferer is a human being. For surely some sufferers, for example, insects, do not have a sufficiently complex conscious-ness to make it possible for them to survive their earthly death. But it does look as though *pace* animal rights advocates, God would not be an unfair utilitarian were he to cause *insects* to suffer in order to keep the suffering of *human beings* at a minimum.

But doesn't Ø entail that not only do I not have an obligation, in normal circumstances, to refrain from causing suffering, but in fact I have an obligation to cause as much suffering as I can, in order to keep the level of suffering at a minimum? The defender of Ø will have to maintain either that God, but not human beings, is such that if *God* did not cause us to suffer as much as we in fact do, then we would suffer still more or that, when it is morally wrong for me to cause suffering, this is because I would be unnecessarily adding to a *minimum* of suffering which is sufficient to prevent still greater suffering. The former reply is preferable to the latter one, which, though it may account for my obligation, in normal circumstances, not to *cause* suffering, it cannot account for the fact that I sometimes have an obligation to abolish suffering which is already occurring.

Still, Ø is in need of considerable defense. For it entails that even a supremely powerful being is such that if he had not caused us to suffer as much as we in fact do, then he could not have prevented us from suffering still more. Even a supremely perfect being cannot falsify a necessary truth – a proposition which is true in all possible worlds. But the claim that it is a necessary truth that if God had not caused us to suffer as much as we in fact do, then he could not have prevented us from suffering still more, surely requires considerable argumentation. I shall return to a discussion of Ø in 3.7 and 3.8.

**2.8**   The claim that suffering is necessary for some enormously valuable end (call it 'E'), which we cannot presently discern, cannot be rejected on the ground that it appears not to be a necessary truth (since E remains unspecified). But the contemplated claim is incompatible with human beings having, in some circumstances, a stringent moral obligation to abolish suffering and, in many circumstances, not to cause it. A related, more plausible claim is that *God's* causing suffering, *qua* cause of the empirical universe, is necessary and sufficient for E, but that this does not hold true of us.

However, there are two reasons for doubting the present solution: (a) It entails that God is an unfair utilitarian unless every sufferer benefits from E. And it is surely doubtful that sentient beings, who are unable to survive their earthly deaths, are benefited by E; (b) T is a very plausible thesis.

**2.9**   I have discussed utilitarian unfairness with respect both to Ø and the E-solution. And it is time to point out that the free will defense as well in effect imputes utilitarian unfairness to God. For, given the free will defense, though you and I enjoy the putative blessing of free will, our choices sometimes result in the suffering of sentient creatures who are not themselves thus benefited.

# 3

# The Argument from Suffering II

3.1 Most theists hold that God is the ground of morality, in the sense that God's pro and con attitudes are constitutive of moral goodness and moral reprehensibility. So the theist holds that if God does not exist, then no one is morally reprehensible, no matter what he does. But the atheistic argument from the suffering of the innocent requires that it be the case that when *human beings* fail to prevent innocent suffering which they can easily prevent, then they are morally reprehensible. And, since the argument's conclusion is that God does not exist, that conclusion is at odds with the envisaged premise; and so it may appear that the argument from suffering is self-undermining.

But the atheist can reply that, even given ethical supernaturalism, a slight reformulation of his argument will show that God does not exist:

(1) *If God exists, then* human beings are morally reprehensible for failing to relieve the suffering of the innocent when they can easily do so.

(2) So, *if* God exists, then *he* is morally reprehensible, since he can easily relieve the suffering of the innocent, but frequently fails to do so.

(3) But, God is, by definition, perfectly moral good: it is a necessary truth that if God exists, then he is *not* morally reprehensible.

(4) Hence, God does not exist.

But the cogency of this argument can be doubted. Let us see why. As we saw in 1.9, the concept of God is such that it is a necessary truth that if God does not exist, then his existence is not logically possible: 'God does not exist' entails 'God's existence is not logically possible. So if God does not exist is true, then it is *true* that God's existence is not logically possible'. And, of course, 'God's existence is not logically possible' entails 'God does not exist'. But 'God's existence is not logically possible' is, if true, a necessary truth. 'God's existence is not logically possible' asserts in effect that it is necessarily false that God exists. And if a proposition is necessarily false in one possible world, then there are no possible worlds in which it is true or even contingent. And any proposition which is entailed by a necessary truth is itself a necessary truth. (If p entails q, then any world in which p is true is a world in which q is true. And if p is a necessary truth, then it, and hence, q, are true in all possible worlds.) So if the argument from suffering establishes that God does not exist, then it establishes *eo ipso* that it is a necessary truth that God does not exist, that is, that God's existence is not logically possible. It follows that if any of the premises of the atheist's argument are epistemically irrelevant to the conclusion that God's existence is logically impossible, then, given that that premise cannot be dispensed with, the atheist's argument is noncogent.

But now the claim that the existence of a given (kind of) thing – for example, a square circle – is logically impossible is normally a *conceptual* claim; and conceptual claims are, if true, justified just in terms of the content of the concepts which they contain: empirical observations are epistemically irrelevant to them. Consider, for example, the following version of a well-known paradox: 'The existence of a male Bostonian barber, who shaves all and only those male Bostonians who don't shave themselves, is logically impossible.' Reflection on the concept of such a barber shows that, if he shaves himself, then he doesn't shave himself, and that, if he doesn't shave himself, then he shaves himself, and, hence, that since he either shaves himself of doesn't shave himself, his existence is logically impossible. But, once again, this conclusion is solely the result of conceptual analysis: empirical observations (of Bostonians or anyone else) are epistemically irrelevant to it.

But, since 'It is a necessary truth that God does not exist' asserts in effect that God's existence is not logically possible, it is, at the very least, likely that it, too, is a conceptual claim. And it follows in turn that it is very likely that the empirical claim that there is widespread suffering of beings, who do not deserve to suffer, is epistemically irrelevant to it. But the atheistic arguer from suffering can hardly dispense with the claim that there is such suffering. Hence, there is reason to think that his argument is noncogent.

It may be objected here that, given my definition of 'a conceptual truth,' it is not a conceptual truth that the contemplated male Bostonian barber cannot exist. For the explanation of the truth of that proposition does not lie precisely in the concept of a male Bostonian barber, who shaves all and only those male Bostonians who don't shave themselves. It lies, rather, in the more abstract concept of an S who X's (for example, kicks) all and only those who don't X themselves.

The objection is well taken, but easily accommodated. The explanation of its being the case that the contemplated barber cannot exist does, indeed, lie in the more abstract concept of an S who X's all and only those who don't X themselves. So we can get the barber paradox under the heading of conceptual truths by defining the latter as truths, the explanation of which lies entirely in precisely the concepts which they contain *or* in more abstract concepts of which the less abstract concepts are instantiations.

But isn't this true of 'If God exists, then he exists'? Doesn't the explanation of that proposition lie in a more abstract concept, of which the concept of God is an instantiation? The answer is that the only candidate for that more abstract concept is the concept of anything. And I submit that it is plain that the concept of anything does not help to explain why it is true that if anything (including God) exists, then it exists.

3.2 By 'p is epistemically relevant to q,' I do not mean that p *deductively entails* q. Every proposition deductively entails a given conceptual (necessary) truth, though not every proposition is epistemically relevant to it. And, anyway, epistemically relevant inductive evidence need not deductively entail its conclusion. Rather, by 'p is epistemically relevant to q relative to a given person, S' I mean that if S's belief that q is caused by her warranted belief that p, then her belief that q is more warranted than it would otherwise be. It follows from this definition that, even if p would be epistemically relevant to q in some epistemic contexts, it is not epistemically relevant to q in case S bases her belief that q on p because p is a member of a set of premises from which S invalidly infers q. By 'S is more epistemically warranted in believing that q than she would otherwise be,' I do not mean that S feels more certain about the truth of q than she would otherwise do. Feeling certain is a subjective, psychological state, which can be produced by things which have nothing to do with epistemic warrant. (Needless to say, I cannot pursue further here the question of the nature of epistemic warrant. Suffice it to say that we have a pre-analytic understanding of epistemic warrant, which surely justifies us in denying that being epistemically warranted in believing that q is the same as feeling certain that q is true.)

3.3   In 1.2, I considered the claim that my thesis that 'God exists' is a nonconditional, ontologically significant proposition, can be cast in doubt by the consideration that all other conceptual truths are reducible to conditionals. Now I think that that claim might well be persuasive, if there were not apparent counter-examples to it, for example, 'The whole number between the number eight and the number ten is odd'.

What I have been arguing in *this* chapter is that, since all other true ascriptions of logical impossibility are conceptual truths, to which empirical claims are epistemically irrelevant, it is very likely that this would hold true of 'God's existence is logically impossible,' were that a true proposition.

But aren't there in fact counter-examples to the thesis that all other true ascriptions of logical impossibility are such that observational evidence is epistemically irrelevant to them? Consider, for example, 'Professor X, who is good at conceptual analysis and a very honest person reports that, upon reflection, she has discovered that the existence of the Bostonian barber mentioned earlier is logically impossible'. This is surely an empirical claim which is, nonetheless, epistemically relevant to the claim that the existence of the contemplated barber is logically impossible.

This objection is well taken, but easily met. Empirical claims which *are* epistemically relevant to ascriptions of logical impossibility are all essentially *testimony* about *non*empirical conceptual analyses.

Here it may be said, 'The empirical truth that "square" means the same as "equilateral rectangle" entails the conceptual truth that squares are rectangles.' Now no doubt this is true, especially in view of the fact that *any* proposition entails the necessary truth that squares are rectangles. But is the envisaged contingent truth *epistemically relevant* to the conceptual truth that squares are rectangles? I submit that it is *not*. We can, of course, imagine a case in which someone doesn't know the meaning of the English word 'square' and/or the English word 'rectangle,' and we tell him that 'rectangle' means 'four-sided figure' and that 'square' means 'equilateral rectangle,' and, in that way, get him to see that the English sentence 'A square is an equilateral rectangle' expresses a conceptual truth. But what we have got him to see is a merely contingent, empirical proposition: it might well *not* have been the case that the envisaged English sentence expresses a necessary truth.

3.4   Quineans will object that there is no hard and fast distinction between what I have been calling 'conceptual truths' and what I have been calling 'empirical truths.' It is just that 'conceptual truths' are more immune to empirical revision than are 'empirical' claims, since the former play an important role in the formation of scientific theories. But since, say, 'No one is a brother of S unless he is a male sibling of S,' and 'No person is a bachelor unless he is unmarried,' obviously play no such role, Quineans must hold that they are no more immune to revision than is, say, 'It's a warm day'. And that certainly appears to be not the case.

3.5   But what exactly is wrong with the argument from suffering? I submit that the answer is that step 2 does not follow from step 1 – that, though moral judgments are universalizable, it does not follow from the fact that any *human* person, who fails to relieve the suffering of the innocent, when he can easily do so, is morally reprehensible for so doing, that any person *simpliciter* is also morally reprehensible for so doing.

This entails that the theodicists whom we considered in Chapter 2, who are in effect asking the question 'What is the morally relevant difference between God and human persons in the envisaged respect?' are, at least, asking the right question. Let us return, then, to the contemplated theodicists.

But first I should point out that the above refutation does not presuppose that my Chapter 1 arguments for the existence of God are sound – only the less controversial claim that if God exists, then his non-existence is not logically possible.

3.6   What precisely follows from the fact that the argument from suffering is a failure? Shall we say that my arguments for that conclusion establish that the free will defense is, after all, a sound rebuttal? Or shall we accept Ø?

I pointed out in 2.10 that the free will defense in effect imputes utilitarian unfairness to God. And I said in 2.8 that it may *look* as if, given that we reject the claim that the envisaged deathbed sufferer survives her earthly death, this is true of Ø as well. But I think that Ø can be made to go through, even if we reject an afterlife, if we specify that the *amount* of suffering which others would undergo, were it not for the suffering of the envisaged deathbed sufferer, is *vastly* greater than the suffering which *she* undergoes.

As the suffering of a given individual, S, which is necessary to prevent suffering on the part of other individuals, is more and more outweighed by the suffering which it prevents, the charge of utilitarian unfairness becomes increasingly less plausible. (I do not mean to endorse the claim that this or that act of wartime terror bombing prevented a great enough amount of future suffering on the part of innocent civilians that it was morally justified. I mean only that it is *conceivable* that an act of terror bombing could be morally justified. I shall return to this topic in the next chapter.)

It follows that Ø, suitably formulated, is superior to the free will defense with respect to the question of utilitarian unfairness.

3.7 Moreover, theists who believe in the efficacy of petitionary prayer will favor Ø over the free will defense. For such theists need to answer the question of why God should relieve (that is, desist from causing) suffering only (or mainly) in answer to prayer.

Consider the case of a suffering atheist, who, through no fault of his own, believes that the sorry state of our world is a good reason for disbelieving in the existence of God, and who therefore never prays. How can it be *fair* of God to relieve the suffering of people who pray to have it relieved and not to relieve the suffering of the innocent atheist?

I submit that the best answer to this question is that God would falsify Ø if he were to relieve suffering which is not prayed about; but that he does not do so when he relieves suffering in answer to prayer. It is of note that the defender of Ø must give a similar answer to the question of why it is frequently morally acceptable (and sometimes morally obligatory) for *human beings* to relieve suffering which is *not* prayed about. That is to say, she must conclude that, though God would falsify Ø under those circumstances, human beings do not.

These answers are, of course, incomplete, since they raise the further question of why a human being's relieving the innocent atheist's suffering would *not* falsify Ø, though God's doing so *would*. Moreover, I think it is clear that we do not know the answer to this question. But it remains true that a partial explanation is better than none at all.

Moreover, the free will defense *per se* does not give us even a partial explanation. According to the free will defender, the best explanation of why God does not intervene to relieve a given instance of suffering, which is due to a wrong choice on the part of either a human or nonhuman moral agent, is that if God *always* thus intervened, then he would make free *right* choices on the part of moral agents impossible, and that there is no nonarbitrary answer to the question, 'Well, then, how often *should* God intervene?' In the case of nondivine moral agents, we should intervene at least on occasions when we can easily do so and the suffering serves no visible good end; but, given the alleged importance of free right choices, this does not hold true of a supremely powerful being.

But this divine motive for not intervening to relieve suffering would obtain whether or not the suffering were prayed about. For whether or not God intervenes in answer to prayer, his intervention *ipso facto* restricts our ability *freely* to refrain from doing harm. So the free will defender, who believes in the efficacy of petitionary prayer, cannot explain why, though God sometimes relieves suffering in answer to prayer, he does not relieve suffering *simpliciter*.

The free will defender may wish to maintain here that people who pray for the relief of suffering deserve to have their suffering relieved to a greater extent than do people who do not pray, since prayer is a virtuous activity. And he might wish to say that the innocent atheist, though innocent, is nonetheless unable to perform these virtuous acts and, hence, does not deserve to have his suffering relieved. But even if this does not seem incredible on the face of it, it cannot account for the putative fact that God sometimes answers the prayers of a given person, $S_1$, for the relief of suffering of *another* person, $S_2$, who does *not* herself engage in prayer.

The free will defender may maintain that his inability to answer the question we have been discussing is not epistemically worse than the inability of the defender of Ø to answer the question of why God would falsify Ø if he were to intervene with respect to the suffering of non-prayerful people. But an inability to answer the former question is *eo ipso* an inability to answer the question of how it can be that God is not unfair vis-à-vis the innocent atheist. And that in turn is an inability to cope with what amounts to a version of the atheistic argument from suffering. But, since the free will defender purports to be giving us an adequate answer to such atheistic arguments, he is committed to giving *some* sort of answer to the contemplated question. And, if he falls back here on a *mix* of the free will defense and Ø, then the question arises as to why explanatory simplicity does not dictate his accepting Ø *simpliciter*.

Here my critic may argue as follows: 'Consider a conditional (call it 'C'), which is essential to Dore's argument: 'If God relieved the suffering of the innocent atheist, then he would falsify Ø.' Dore is committed to holding that since, in view of God's supreme goodness, the consequent of this conditional is necessarily false, so, too, is its antecedent. But then the latter entails *every* proposition, including the proposition that God would *not* falsify Ø. So Dore's explanation of why God does not relieve the suffering of the innocent atheist is, in reality, a pseudo-explanation.'

The point is well taken, but we can reformulate C as follows: 'If the theist who believes in petitionary prayer *had reason to believe* that God relieved the suffering of the innocent atheist, then he *would have reason to believe* that God, if he exists, had falsified Ø, and, hence, since, if God exists, then he is necessarily good, he *would have reason to believe* that God does not exist.' It is clear that neither the consequent nor the antecedent of this conditional (call it 'C' ) is necessarily false. And it is also clear that C' is all that the defender of Ø requires in order to explain why *it is rational* for us to believe my explanation of why God does not relieve the suffering of the innocent atheist.

Thus far I have been discussing the question of why God relieves suffering only in answer to petitionary prayer. But there is, of course, another pertinent question, namely, why does God frequently *fail* to answer that kind of prayer? People who deny that petitionary prayer is sometimes efficacious may not be satisfied with the reply that God answers all prayers for the relief of suffering, which are such that his answering them does not falsify Ø. For they may want to maintain that the fact that many prayers go unanswered is evidence that those prayers which the theist takes to be answered are merely randomly accompanied by a reduction of suffering.

And there is this much to be said about that claim: The theist who affirms the efficacy of petitionary prayer needs to reflect on the following question: are there series of prayers which are such that it is highly improbable that they are only randomly accompanied by a reduction of suffering? It would be a mistake to think that the answer is *obviously* 'No,' in view of all those prayers which go unanswered. Even if the last 50 flips of the coin have conformed to a normal probability curve, the next 50 flips randomly yielding 50 heads in a row is highly improbable. Of course, in the latter case it is *possible* to discover that in fact this series has been randomly produced. In the case of the putative answering by God of a series of prayers, however, it is far from clear how (in this life) we could discover that in fact they were only randomly accompanied by a reduction of suffering. So if the reflective theist answers the envisaged question affirmatively, the non-prayerful skeptic is not in a position to gainsay her.

3.8  Let us return briefly to the free will defense. In 2.7, I maintained that a necessary condition of being able freely to refrain from raping children is not being psychologically compelled not to do so, that is not being a compulsive non-raper. And I suggested that that is not a good condition to be in.

Now suppose that in fact it is better than not that we be compulsive non-wrongdoers *simpliciter*. Then since there are free wrong actions, not only is it not *better* than not that we have free will, it is *worse* than not that we have it. And that is another reason for holding that our having free will is a *part* of the problem of evil, rather than a successful *solution* of it. It follows that the answer to the question of why we have a capacity for freely harming one another must be in terms of the Ø solution, rather than being its competitor.

None of this entails, of course, that we do not *have* such a capacity, nor that those who exercise it do not deserve to suffer as a consequence.

3.9  Someone may object here that I am committed to the conclusion that human beings have a perfection which God lacks, namely, the power to end the suffering of the innocent atheist without doing what is morally wrong. But since, given the Ø-solution, that power would be a *defect* in God, his *having* that power does not count as a perfection which he lacks, that is, as a property which would, if he possessed it, make him more perfect than in fact he is.

Another objection is that God's being unable to abolish the suffering of the innocent atheist without falsifying Ø, and, hence, doing what is seriously wrong, is a *defect* in God, and, indeed, a defect from which many human beings do not suffer. But it follows from the fact that we have reason to believe that God exists and is supremely perfect, that the argument from suffering is noncogent, and that the best explanation of precisely what is wrong with it is the Ø solution; that the envisaged putative defect is, despite appearances, not, on balance, a defect, since it is a necessary condition of God's having some indiscernible perfection which is such that he is, on balance, more perfect than he would be if he lacked it.

I have been arguing that it is a necessary truth that God cannot relieve suffering without even more suffering resulting, except in answer to prayer. And, since God is the cause of the empirical universe, this entails that it is a necessary truth that God *cannot desist from causing suffering* without his causing even more suffering. And that entails in turn that God cannot desist from causing suffering *simpliciter*. But can it really be the case that such a being is supremely perfect? Can it be true that being unable to desist from causing suffering is such that it is better than not that God possesses that property?

One answer is that we do not know all of the perfections which are possessed by a supremely perfect being, and that it may well be that, in the context of *all* of those perfections, being unable to desist from causing suffering *is* a perfection. And, even setting that consideration aside, it is open to the ontological arguer of Chapter 1 to point out that the arguments there can be made to go through if we simply stipulate that God is, *in all other respects*, a supremely perfect being.

It is of note that the free will defender can give a similar answer to the objection that, given the cogency of the free will defense, God lacks a perfection which some human beings have, namely, being able to perform free right actions (since it is a conceptual truth that he does not engage in wrongdoing). The arguments of Chapter 1 will go through even if the free will defender concedes this, but adds that God is supremely perfect *in all other respects*.

Here it may be objected that, once the ontological arguer starts qualifying in this way, it is merely arbitrary of him to refuse to include existence in the list of exceptions. But a plausible reply is that (1) there is a *prima facie* case on behalf of none of those exceptions obtaining and (2) though our observations of suffering, and our reflections on the concept of a supremely perfect being, overthrows that *prima facie* case, with respect to the putative perfections of being able to desist from causing suffering and being able freely to avoid wrongdoing, it does *not* overthrow that *prima facie* case with respect to God's existence, since, as we have seen, the argument from suffering against the *existence* of God is noncogent; and reflection on the concept of a supremely perfect being shows that he exists rather than that he does not exist.

3.10 It is of note that Ø is highly compatible with a plausible interpretation of the Christian doctrine of the Vicarious Atonement. Since many people no longer believe in the spiritual efficacy of blood sacrifice and in scapegoatism (even voluntary scapegoatism), and since most reputable Bible scholars agree that the Bible is not an accurate historical document, many contemporary people, who want to be part of the Christian tradition, must treat the doctrine of the Vicarious Atonement as myth-cum-metaphor. And I submit that the best way to understand that metaphor is in terms of Ø: Christ is mankind suffering so that mankind will not have to suffer still more. On this interpretation the Christian Trinity becomes (a) God, *qua* the uncreated Creator of everything else (God the Father), (b) God *qua* becoming mankind and suffering so that mankind need not suffer still more (Christ), and (c) God *qua* sustainer of the Christian tradition (the Holy Spirit). Moreover, nonfundamentalist Christians may want to stay even closer to the tradition by professing, as an item of faith, that the reason that we would suffer still more than we do, if we did not in fact suffer as much as we do, is that Adam and Eve (that is, human beings, in general) have engaged in moral wrongdoing.

Here it may be said that the concept of God becoming identical with mankind is logically incoherent, since God is necessarily the transcendent creator of mankind. But I am not suggesting that God actually *has* the property of having become one with his creation. I am claiming only that this is a *metaphorical* characterization of God. And, of course, metaphors very frequently fail to conform to the laws of logic.

An argument against a literalistic interpretation of the doctrine of the Trinity is that, as we saw in 1.7, God is incorporeal, but Christ (Jesus of Nazareth) was, if he existed, corporeal. Thomas Morris tries to take this apparent discrepancy into consideration by maintaining that Jesus is not God *simpliciter*, but rather God the Son. [1] Morris writes that orthodoxy does not allege any historical man to be identical with God *simpliciter* . . . the identity claim made about Christ in the doctrine of the Incarnation is . . . Jesus is God the Son, not Jesus is God (pp. 20–1).

But if Morris is willing to affirm that God the Father and God the Son (and God the Holy Spirit) *are* identical with one another, then part of what he is affirming is that, though Jesus is corporeal, and God the Father is not, nonetheless Jesus is God the Son and God the Son is God the Father. And, given the transitivity of identity and Leibniz's law, this is a necessary falsehood. Morris is obliged to conclude, then, that God the Son and God the Father are distinct individuals. On pp. 207–8, Morris says that he is 'inclined to endorse a Social Trinitarianism' which he defines as follows:

[T]he deity worshipped by Christians is comprised by three ontologically distinct persons, severally exemplifying each of the attributes strictly necessary for being God, or for being literally divine.

But I think that by conceding that Jesus of Nazareth is not identical with God, Morris has not, in fact, left himself an option.

What shall we think of Social Trinitarianism? The answer is that it is incompatible with a successful critique of the various parodies of the ontological argument which we considered in 1.4.

The claim that each individual member of the Social Trinity is the uncreated created creator of everything else, including the other members of the Social Trinity, is obviously logically absurd. Suppose, then, that the Social Trinitarian maintains instead that the three members of the Trinity are *partners* in the creative process, though no one of them is *individually* the creator of everything else. Then, since the Social Trinitarian has conceded that there is more than *one* individual who is the creator of everything other than those individuals, he needs to tell us why the ontological argument cannot be used to establish the existence of, say, a billion such individuals. The rejoinder that only *divine* individuals can be cooperators in the creative process simply raises the further question of why, given that there is more than *one* divine individual, there can be only *three* such individuals.

Consider minor deities, once again, that is, beings who have all of God's perfections except . . . , where 'existence' is not a tautology-making fill in. My way of coping with the concept of minor deities was to maintain that, no matter how many dots we might fill in, the vast majority of God's perfections would remain unmentioned and, hence, that the concept of minor deities is the concept of beings who rival God with respect to the *number* of his perfections, and so is logically incoherent.

But if the ontological answer were to grant that there is an individual, namely, God the Father, who can be rivaled, with respect to the number of his perfections by two *other* individuals, namely, God the Son and God the Holy Spirit, then he would owe us an explanation of why it should be the case that it is logically impossible for any *other* individual so to rival God the Father. And, if he said that the three members of the Trinity are divine individuals and that it is logically impossible for any *non*divine individual to rival any *divine* individual with respect to the number of his perfections; then, again, he would be obliged to show that, even though there are *three* divine individuals, it is logically impossible for there to be (many) *more* than three.

Perhaps Morris will say here 'So much the worse for the ontological argument.' But, in that case, he owes the ontological arguer a cogent refutation of it. And if he says that the parodies of 1.4 constitute such a refutation, then since, given the ontological argument, the parodies fail, he will be begging the question. Moreover, he will owe us an explanation, which does not make reference to the soundness of the ontological argument, of precisely what *is* wrong with the parodies.

3.11  A simpler solution of the problem of suffering, though one which does not throw light on Christian doctrine, is that God is unable to abolish suffering *simpliciter* (except, perhaps, in answer to prayer). The question of whether this is a defect in God can be answered in a manner similar to the answer to the earlier question of whether it is a defect in God that he cannot abolish the suffering which we in fact undergo without causing even more suffering (except, perhaps, in answer to prayer): the envisaged divine inability is not, on balance, a defect since it is a necessary condition of God's having some indiscernible perfection which is such that he is, on balance, more perfect than he would be if he lacked it.

In the end, however, I think that the Ø-solution can be seen to be superior to the solution which we are now contemplating. For, unlike the Ø-solution, it does not provide us with an explanation of *why* God would not be *more* perfect than in fact he is, if he had the envisaged power. Given the Ø-solution, God would be *less* perfect than in fact he is if he had the power to abolish suffering, except, perhaps, in answer to prayer. For that power would be the power to do what is seriously wrong. And God's having the power to do what is seriously wrong would *diminish* his perfection.

For those who think that it would be a perfection in God to have that power and *freely to refrain from exercising it*, there is another answer: It is, as we saw in Chapter 1, a conceptual truth that God exists, *qua* supremely morally good, that is, it is *necessarily false* that God exercises the envisaged power, and, hence, it is necessarily false that he has it. It follows that his not having that power is a necessary condition of God's very existence, and that, since his having it would be incompatible with his existence, it could not possibly be perfection-increasing.

# 4

# How God Grounds
# Morality I

4.1 Many philosophers, including Plato and Hobbes, have held that it is in a person's overriding interest that he conform his behavior to moral obligations, and that its being in his overriding interest to do so entails his being significantly harmed if he does not. Suppose that these philosophers are right in thinking that the overridingness of morality is thus connected with harm. (I shall argue that they are in 4.3 through 4.7.) Then a simple argument that we do not have moral obligations unless God exists can be constructed. Another feature of the concept of a moral obligation is that if I have a moral obligation to refrain from performing a given action, then anyone who is relevantly similar to me also has that obligation. Moreover, merely being much shrewder than I and, hence, being able to avoid human detection is *not* a morally relevant difference between you and me; and, neither is your being able to avoid human punishment by being much more *powerful* than I. Indeed, no matter how shrewd and powerful an individual might be – no matter whether he is *vastly* shrewder and more powerful than any human being – this would not constitute a morally relevant difference with respect to him and a less shrewd and powerful person: if the latter had a given moral obligation and the former did not have it, then this could not be just because of the envisaged degree of shrewdness and power. But there must be something which guarantees that, not only would a human being be significantly harmed for failing to fulfill that obligation, but so, too, would *any* moral agent, no matter how shrewd and powerful he might be. (I do not mean to endorse the claim that there are in fact superhuman putative moral reprobates, only that they are possible.) And this entails that, given that we have moral obligations, there must be a supremely knowledgeable and supremely powerful being who enforces them. Moreover, being such an enforcer would be one of the perfections in virtue of which a being would be supremely perfect. And, just as the concept of a supremely perfect being is such that no other being can be the uncreated creator of everything else (see 1.6) so, too, the concept of a supremely perfect being is such that no other being can have the presently contemplated perfection. It follows that if there are moral obligations, then God exists.

My point here can be reexpressed as follows: If God does not exist, then the superhuman putative reprobates whom we have been contemplating would not have moral obligations. But, since being superhuman, with respect to power and shrewdness, would not be a morally relevant difference between them and ordinary human beings, it follows that if God does not exist, then ordinary human beings do not have moral obligations.

It may look as if, given that philosophers like Plato and Hobbes are right, then human beings have moral obligations, regardless of whether God exists. Plato's most ambitious attempt to show that it is strongly in the interest of every person to avoid wrongdoing is in *The Republic*, where he argues on behalf of a tripartite soul which inevitably suffers as a result of wrongdoing and *a fortiori* which suffers, regardless of whether God exists. But whatever may be thought of the structure of the personalities of actual wrongdoers, it is surely *possible* for there to be wrongdoers whose personalities are *not* thus structured. And, in particular, it is surely *possible* that there be superhuman wrongdoers whose personalities are *not* such that for them to do wrong is *ipso facto* for them to suffer, regardless of whether God exists.

Hobbes held that the fulfilling of moral obligations *by human beings* is a necessary condition of their leading a tolerable life, since the alternative is a state of affairs in which every human being suffers at the hands of other human beings. And he might well have said of the superhuman moral agents whom I have been discussing that, indeed, they would not have moral obligations. But the trouble with *that* concession is that, in view of the universalizability of judgments about moral obligations, and in view of the fact that great power and shrewdness do not constitute a morally relevant difference between those who possess them and those who do not, what follows from the envisaged conclusion is that no one, including no human being, has, in fact, any moral obligations.

Another objection is that we do not *require* a supremely powerful-and-knowledgeable being to guarantee that the envisaged superhuman reprobates are harmed, since, as I argued in 1.4, no other being can possibly even begin to *rival* God with respect to power and knowledge, and, hence, no superhuman reprobates could possibly be powerful and shrewd enough so that only a *supremely* powerful and knowledgeable being could guarantee that they are harmed. But the answer is simply that what I maintained in effect is that no other being can rival God (only) *if God exists*. Here my central argument can be restated:

(1)  If God does not exist, then the envisaged superhuman putative wrongdoers could have enough power and shrewdness so that only a supremely powerful-cum-knowledgeable being could punish them.
(2)  Hence, if God does not exist, then these superhuman putative wrongdoers are possible.
(3)  But, as I have argued, if they are possible then human beings have no moral obligations.
(4)  So, if God does not exist, then human beings have no moral obligations.

4.2  Someone may object that it is also true that if God does not exist, then some *other* being can have the perfection of being the envisaged moral enforcer. But I submit that morality presupposes that retributive, as opposed to utilitarian, punishment for wrong-doing be *just*, and that retribution is unjust if the person who engages in it is to some extent morally imperfect. Hence, if the envisaged enforcer engages in retributive punishment, then he is both supremely powerful, supremely knowledgeable and supreme-ly morally good. And I submit that no other being could rival a supremely perfect being with respect to those properties.

But why should we suppose that the envisaged moral enforcer engages in *retributive* punishment? Why should we not think that he is a utilitarian? The answer is simply that the utilitarian theory of punishment is that restraint and/or deterrence justify punishment. But, if the contemplated supremely perfect moral enforcer does not exist, then it is possible for there to be beings who are sufficiently powerful and knowledgeable so that no one can restrain and/or deter them. And beings who cannot be restrained and/or deterred would be such that utilitarianism entails that it would be morally *wrong* to harm them, if, indeed, that were possible. But utilitarianism also entails that if it would be morally wrong to harm them, then they are not morally reprehensible. And, once again, that entails that none of us is.

Here it may be said that harming the contemplated superhuman putative wrongdoers might deter *human beings* from engaging in wrongdoing. But the answer is simply that it might not and, indeed, would not if, as is possible, we knew nothing about that harm.

4.3  So far, I have been assuming that the overridingness of moral obligations entails their being such that those who violate them will be significantly harmed. One very good reason for doing so is this: Since some moral obligations can, in specific contexts, override *other* moral obligations, it will not do merely to characterize moral obligations as overriding *simpliciter*. And, of course, it would be unhelpfully circular to characterize moral obligations as being overriding with respect to everything *other* than moral obligations. Moreover, my supernaturalistic account can easily solve this problem. Given my account, we have only to say that any moral obligation to perform a given action, $A_1$, is such that an individual, S, who has that obligation will be punished by God for failing to do $A_1$, unless there is some other action, $A_2$, which is such that (1) S cannot perform both $A_1$ and $A_2$ and (2) God is disposed to punish S for not performing $A_2$ rather than for not performing $A_1$.

Here it may be said that this entails that God is not after all a just being, since in some instances of conflicting obligations, it is not clear to the individual who has them which obligation it is which he should fulfill. But the ethical supernaturalist can accommodate *this* consideration by the simple expedient of pointing out that, in those cases, one obligation rather than another is *not* overriding relative to S: though it is of overriding importance to him that he fulfill one *or* the other, it is not of overriding importance that he fulfill specifically this one or that one.

4.4  A noncircular account of the nature of the overridingness of morality, other than the one which is set out in 4.3, relativizes morality to individuals in the following way: P is a moral principle relative to an individual, S, if and only if S would let P override any other action-guiding principle, or S would feel remorse at not doing so. But this is obviously inadequate; for there are sometimes conflicts between principles of *prima facie* moral obligation which are such that it is obvious to S that one principle (for example, 'One has a *prima facie* moral obligation not to cause great suffering'), should override the other (for example, 'One has a *prima facie* moral obligation not to tell deliberate falsehoods'), and, hence, in which S is rightly convinced that he is doing the right thing, all things considered, in not acting on the latter principle, and so correctly feels no remorse at all for not doing so.

Can we make do, then, with the following characterization: 'P is a principle of *prima facie* moral obligation relative to S if and only if either S will feel remorse if he does not act on P or he will have what he takes to be an adequate justification for not acting on it'? The answer is 'No' for two reasons: (1) At least one justification for not acting on a principle of *prima facie* moral obligation on a given occasion is that it conflicts with another such principle on that occasion, so the envisaged characterization is circular; (2) It is highly implausible that S would be justified in maintaining that, for example, 'There is a *prima facie* moral obligation not to take innocent human life' does not express a moral judgment solely on the ground that he would not feel any remorse for not acting on it, even in a case in which there was no conflicting principle.

Nor will it do to elaborate on the contemplated account as follows: 'P is a *prima facie* moral principle relative to S if and only if, given that S is not justified in not acting on it, S would feel remorse for not doing so *or ought to feel remorse.*' Since the 'ought' here is the moral 'ought,' the envisaged characterization is circular.

4.5 In his book, *Moral Thinking*, R. M. Hare gives the following account of the overridingness of moral principles: P is a moral principle relative to a given individual, S, if and only if either (a) S would let P take precedence over any P-violating course of action which he might consider, or (b) where P is not such a principle, 'critical thinking, however primitive' about P would lead S to justify P by appealing to at least one principle which S does treat as overriding, and, hence, is for S a moral principle.[1]

One reason for rejecting Hare's characterization is this: There may in fact be a few moral principles which cannot be overridden by any other moral principles. 'It is wrong for a person to torture and kill unwilling victims, when his only motive is a desire for sexual gratification, and he is able to refrain from acting on that motive' appears to be an example. But is it really the case that *every* overridable moral principle can be defended by reference to such an absolute, nonoverridable principle? Hare does not furnish examples, but surely we need them.

But there is another, more basic objection to Hare's view, as well as to all attempts to relativize overridingness, and, hence, the concept of morality, to individuals. Consider 'S is morally obliged to do X'. Suppose that S refuses to treat this judgment as overriding or as justifiable by a judgment which S takes to be overriding. Does it really make any sense to say that, relative to S, the former judgment is not a *moral* judgment? An affirmative answer here is surely as implausible as the claim that, say, 'A trade war would be harmful to the economies of the nations involved' is not an economic judgment, relative to S, if he refuses to take it as an economic judgment. Just as we pick out economic judgments syntactically-cum-semantically, so we pick out moral judgments syntactically-cum-semantically, that is, in terms of words like 'morally obliged'. And it is surely incredible that 'S is morally obliged to do X' has its syntax and semantics only relative to individuals who are or are not willing to treat it as overriding or, at least, justifiable, relative to some judgment which they treat as overriding.

I am not here abandoning my claim that overridingness is closely connected with moral obligation. My view is, rather, that *true* moral judgments are such that it is of overriding importance to persons that they conform their behavior to those judgments, regardless of whether they are strongly inclined to do to do. But moral judgments *per se* are, whether true or false, *picked out* in terms of syntax and semantics, not in terms of whether a given individual is inclined to treat them as moral judgments.

4.6 It should be emphasized here that the thesis that the overridingness of morality with respect to a moral agent consists of its being of overriding importance *to her* that she fulfill her moral obligations does not entail that the only, or even the best, *reason* for her to do so is that she will be significantly harmed if she does not. Perhaps the best – in the sense of 'most admirable' – reason which she can give for doing so is that otherwise *other people* will be significantly harmed. Still, if the judgment that she *ought* to do such and such is a true *moral* judgment, then in fact she herself will be harmed for failing to fulfill it.

An analogy may make this clearer. It may be that the best reason for my conforming my conduct to some true economic judgment is that I will benefit people if I do. But the fact that I will be doing that is not what makes the judgment an economic judgment, but rather that it is about the acquisition and/or transfer of goods. And similar considerations hold for scientific judgments. The best reason for me not to jump off the roof may be that, because of gravity, I will be injured if I do. But it is not in virtue of that fact that the judgment that I will fall as a result of gravity is specifically a scientific judgment. And so on for *aesthetic* judgments, and so on. In brief, the present characterization of the nature of morality is not intended to be an *egoistic* theory of moral *reasons*.

At the end of the Roman Catholic Act of Contrition, the penitent says, 'I detest all my sins because I dread the loss of heaven and the pains of hell; but most of all because they offend thee, O my God, who art all good and deserving of all my love'. A person who utters these words sincerely is said to have made a Perfect Act of Contrition, and that is said to be sufficient for his avoiding divine punishment after death. But Catholic priests sometimes advise the faithful that sinners may well not be able to say this prayer sincerely.


4.7   There may perhaps be people who apply the terms 'morally right' and 'morally wrong' to actions which are such that it is not in the overriding interest of a moral agent that she perform them or refrain from performing them. Fibbing (telling a 'white lie') is an example. But the reason why, for some people, this kind of action is taken to be a breach of morality is simply that (a) it involves the telling of a deliberate falsehood and (b) there are many contexts in which that activity causes significant harm and, hence, is such that it *is* of overriding importance to a moral agent that she not engage in it. To the extent that fibbing and other such actions fall under the heading of morality or immorality, they should, therefore, be labeled 'derivatively moral or immoral' and not thought of as exceptions to the thesis that it is of overriding importance to any moral agent that she fulfill her *non*-derivative moral obligations.


4.8   I said in 2.7 that I would return to the question of whether it is at all plausible that human moral agents survive their earthly deaths. I think that we are now in a position to see that the answer is 'Yes'. For it is clearly false that all human moral reprobates suffer *in this life* to at least as great an extent as do the relatively morally innocent. But aren't our bodies-cum-brains perishable? And isn't the mind dependent upon (if not identical with) bodies-cum-brains? I shall return to these questions in Appendix II.

4.9   Predestinationist Christians hold that God punishes human beings for doing what they were not free to fail to do. Or, at any rate, they hold this, unless they believe that all human beings are identical with Adam and Eve, about whom he believes that they fell of their own free will. And the latter is surely not literally (nonmetaphorically) true.

Here a predestinationist may argue as follows: 'The theist who objects to predestinationism can be met by *tu quoque*. For he is aware of the fact that, say, innocent children starve to death, and, since he is a theist, he believes that God, a supremely good and powerful being, permits this to happen, though he could easily do otherwise, even though human beings, who can easily prevent some of the starvation of the innocent, are morally reprehensible for failing to do so. So why should the nonpredestinationist theist be concerned about the claim that, though God is perfectly good, he punishes sinners who could not have done other than sin? No doubt, human beings who punish people for doing what they could not help doing are morally culpable. But it no more follows from this that if God exists, then he, too, is morally culpable for punishing the innocent, than it follows from the fact that human beings are reprehensible for failing to prevent the starvation of an innocent child, when they can easily prevent it, that God is blameworthy as well.'

But the nonpredestinationist has a reply: 'We have numerous examples of people justifiably inflicting pain on other people and/or permitting them to suffer in order to realize some valuable end. So it is not simply *self-evident* that God does not justifiably cause and/or permit suffering for some good purpose (though, perhaps, one which we cannot discern in this life). However, we have no examples of someone, $S_1$, justifiably punishing another person, $S_2$, solely for the reason that $S_2$ behaved in such and such a way, when $S_1$ knows that $S_2$ could not have done otherwise. And I submit that we can know *a priori* that we will never encounter such examples, that is, that it is self-evident that it is seriously wrong to punish people for that reason. So we can know *a priori* that if God, a morally perfect being, exists, then predestinationism is false.'

It is of note that the predestinationist is committed to the conclusion that, since no sinner can do other than sin, human beings, when they deliberately punish sinners are deliberately punishing innocent people – or, at any rate, that predestinationists (who allegedly know that sinners are innocent) are so doing. But deliberately participating in the punishment of innocent people is surely seriously wrong.

I am assuming here that it is possible to punish people for doing what they cannot help doing, that is, that it is possible to punish morally innocent people. And a particularly fastidious philosopher may maintain that in fact the meaning of 'punishing a person' is, roughly, 'inflicting suffering on that person because (a) he did what would have been seriously morally wrong if he was able to do otherwise, and (b) he was, in fact, able to do otherwise'. If this is correct, then it is logically impossible to punish an innocent person.

In reply, my ear for ordinary language tells me that the contemplated definition is incorrect. (Is it really the case that an innocent person could not be punished by the judicial system for a crime which he didn't commit?) And, at any rate, I can reformulate my argument as follows: 'If predestinationism is correct, then predestinationists sometimes participate in inflicting suffering on people for doing things about which the predestinationist knows that they are powerless to do otherwise; and *that* is seriously wrong.'

# 5

# How God Grounds
# Morality II

5.1 Let us call being for something 'a pro-attitude' and being against something a 'con-attitude'. And let us label ethical theories, which maintain that our positive and negative moral judgments have to do with pro and con attitudes respectively, 'attitude theories'.

I submit that it is obvious that attitude theories, thus broadly characterized, are on the right track if any ethical theories are, and, hence, that if none of them is true, then morality is an illusion. In what follows I shall be doing two things: (a) defending attitude theories in general against some more or less standard objections and (b) defending a theistic version of one kind of attitude theory namely, the so-called 'Ideal Observer Theory'.

5.2 One objection to attitude theories in general is that an adequate explication of our pro and con attitudes reveals that the belief that something, X, is good is an essential constituent of a pro-attitude toward X and that the belief that X is bad is an essential constituent of a con-attitude toward X, and that, hence, attitude theories are viciously circular. But in fact it is very doubtful that pro and con attitudes are thus essentially cognitive. A parent may love an offspring whom she knows is a thoroughly bad person and hate an enemy of the latter, even though she believes that he is good.

5.3 There have been three kinds of widely discussed attitude theories. (1) Cultural Relativism – the theory that the moral goodness or badness of X is relative to a majority of people in a given culture having pro or con attitudes toward X. (2) Egoistic Relativism – the theory that the moral goodness or badness of X is relative to the attitude toward X of a given individual. (3) The Ideal Observer Theory – the theory that goodness and badness have to do

51

with the attitudes of a qualified moral judge. (I shall explicate the later concept presently.)

It has, until recently, been held that all three theories are semantic theories, that is, theories of the *meaning* of 'good' and 'bad'. If this is so, then any one of them can be rejected if, in fact it does not yield a *bona fide* definition of those words. Thus, the semantic version of Cultural Relativism can be rejected on the ground that a moral reformer can say without inconsistency that even though a majority of people in her culture have a pro-attitude toward X, the latter is nonetheless morally bad. And similar considerations hold for 'X is morally bad'. Moreover, with respect to Egoistic Relativism, the semantic version is mistaken, since a person can say without inconsistency, for example, 'I know that it would be morally wrong of you not to confess to the crime, but I abhor the thought of your doing so, because I desperately want you to stay out of prison'. Moreover, this consideration applies both to what can be called *descriptivist* Egocentric Relativism and *nondescriptivist* varieties of that theory. The former view has it that when a speaker says 'X is morally good' she is reporting that she has a pro-attitude toward X, and that when she says 'X is morally bad' she is reporting that she has a con-attitude toward X. Nondescriptivism, on the other hand, asserts that 'X is morally good' and 'X is morally bad' make evident that the speaker has a pro or con attitude toward X, without reporting that she does, as one's wincing makes evident that she is in pain, without reporting that she is in pain. But, though this has been frequently overlooked, if nondescriptivism were correct, then 'I agree that it would be morally wrong of you not to confess to the crime, but I desperately want you not to' would be like shouting 'Bravo for X' and adding that X is disgusting, that is, though it would not be, strictly speaking, inconsistent, it would embody a gross linguistic infelicity. And since there are contexts in which it would not do the latter, semantical nondescriptivism is patently false. It is, perhaps, less clear that 'A qualified moral judge would have a pro (or con) attitude toward X, but X is nonetheless morally bad (or good)' embodies an inconsistency. But, in any case, we need not treat the Ideal Observer Theory or indeed, Cultural and Descriptivist Egocentric Relativism as definitions of 'morally good' and 'morally bad'. Instead we can treat them as nonsemantical theories of the *nature* of moral goodness and the nature of moral badness. An appropriate analogy is the claim that volumes *of water* are in reality swarms of $H_2O$ molecules. Someone who supposed that this is a semantical theory of the meaning of the English word, 'water,' rather than a theory of the *nature* of water, would be correctly thought to be confused. And what I am suggesting here is that the attitude theorist, as opposed to the chemist, can also maintain that his theory is nonsemantical. (Nondescriptivist Egoistic Relativism is, however, an exception, that is, it is essentially a semantical theory, for nondescriptive utterances cannot refer to states of affairs which are constitutive of goodness and badness.) In 5.8 I shall offer a definition (that is, a *semantic* theory) of 'morally bad,' and 'morally good'.

However, nonsemantical Cultural Relativism cannot accommodate the moral reformer, but must treat him as essentially similar to the person who *denies* that volumes of water are swarms of $H_2O$ molecules, a thesis which entails that all moral reformers (for example, King and Gandhi) are remarkably obtuse. And the nonsemantical Egoistic Relativist must maintain that a person who says 'I strongly favor your not doing it, though I know that it would be morally wrong of you not to do it' is analogous to a person who says 'It is not a swarm of $H_2O$ molecules, though I know that it is a volume of water'. A further objection to nonsemantical Egoistic Relativism will emerge shortly.

5.4   Let us turn, then, to the Ideal Observer Theory (the IOT for short). And let us construe it as a nonsemantical theory of the nature of moral goodness and badness, namely the theory that X is morally good (or bad) if a person who was completely well informed and vividly imaginative about X and its consequences, as well as completely impartial with respect to X and its consequences would have a pro (or con) attitude toward X. The IOT does not suffer from the defects of the other attitude theories which I have been discussing, since (1) it can accommodate moral reformers by the simple expedient of maintaining that the moral reformer is committed only to the thesis that what he is opposed to is not something toward which *an ideal observer* would have a pro-attitude; and (2) it can accommodate the fact that I may believe that it would be morally bad of you not to confess to the crime, even though I am opposed to your doing it, by maintaining that *an ideal observer* would not be opposed.

5.5   An objection to the IOT is that, since not all qualified human moral judges always exhibit the same pro or con attitudes toward something, X, we are never warranted in inferring that an ideal observer – someone who is as qualified a moral judge as it is possible to be – would in fact have a pro or con attitude toward X. The objection can be stated thusly: The IO theorist typically maintains that we are warranted in making an inductive inference from the fact that qualified human observers of X have a pro or con attitude toward X, to the hypothetical conclusion that a completely qualified observer of X would also have a pro or con attitude toward X. Now I think that in fact it is the case that it happens for the most part that equally knowledgeable, imaginative and impartial human judges form similar attitudes towards X. But, again, this does not always happen. An example of a discrepancy between qualified human judges is embodied, I think, in the conflicting attitudes toward the massive bombing and killing of innocent civilians (for example, children) during wartime. Qualified human judges who look favorably on these actions base their attitudes on the consideration that it is likely that they prevent an even greater, future loss of innocent human life. Qualified human judges who strongly oppose these actions normally maintain that omitting to save innocent human life in wartime is better than taking it unless the amount of innocent suffering which is prevented outweighs the suffering which is inflicted to a much greater extent than is in fact the case. And the inductivist IO theorist cannot adequately account for such a case. For he is committed by his inductivism to the thesis that some ideal observers would have a pro-attitude toward the envisaged actions and some would have a con-attitude, that is, he is committed to the conclusion that those actions would be both morally good and morally bad. (Or, in case he inductively infers an *indifferent* ideal observer as well, he is committed to the conclusion that they would be morally good and morally bad and neither.)

But this kind of relativism is unacceptable in a nonsemantical, moral theory. Let us return to Egoistic Relativism for a moment. *Qua* semantical theory, it can easily account for disagreements among moral judges. For, on that view, my saying that X is morally good and your saying that it is morally bad simply amounts to my saying that I have a positive attitude toward X and your saying that you have a negative attitude; and, hence, there is no appearance here of logical inconsistency. However, if the Egoistic Relativist says instead that my pro-attitude toward X is *constitutive* of its moral goodness, as a swam of $H_2O$ molecules is constitutive of a given volume of water, and that your con-attitude toward X is similarly constitutive of its moral badness, then we do not have here a mere appearance of inconsistency, but, rather, the real thing. It is as if one should maintain that a given object is both made entirely out of lead and entirely out of plastic. And similar considerations hold for the nonsemantical IOT. The conclusion that some IO's would *favor* X while still others would *disfavor* it or be indifferent to it is, given that these facts are nonsemantically constitutive of X's being morally good and morally bad or neither, is like the conclusion that an object is made entirely out of gold and entirely out of silver. It is, of course, possible that an object is made *partly* out of gold and *partly* out of silver. But here the analogy breaks down. For it would surely be absurd to maintain that X is (only) partly good (because at least one IO would favor it) and (only) partly bad (because at least one IO would disfavor it) and (only) partly neither (because at least one IO would be indifferent to it).

But why should the IO theorist accept a nonsemantical version of his theory? Why shouldn't he maintain instead that 'X is morally good (or bad)' just *means* 'Some ideal observer would favor (or disfavor) X'? Then 'X is good and bad (and, perhaps, neither good nor bad)' would, despite first appearances, not be logically inconsistent. For it is perfectly possible that one ideal observer would favor X and that another would disfavor it (and that still another would be indifferent to it).

The answer is that semantical versions of the IOT cannot account for morally sensitive opponents of intentionally taking innocent human life at, say, Nagasaki. For imagine that a semantical IO theorist argues as follows: 'You hold that the intentional taking of innocent human life there was morally wrong. But Jones, who is just as qualified a moral judge as your are, supposes that it had a utilitarian justification. So we should infer that some IO's would have a con-attitude toward what happened there and that some would not. Hence, it was both morally unacceptable and morally acceptable.' It is surely true that if a morally sensitive person rejected this argument, we would not *ipso facto* be warranted in believing just that he doesn't know the meaning of 'morally acceptable' and 'morally unacceptable'. Nor would he necessarily dogmatically contend that no human being who disagrees with him is a qualified moral judge.

5.6 I shall presently formulate a sound nonsemantical version of the IOT. But first it is of note that if there is such a version, then we have in effect an adequate account of the nature of evidence for our moral judgments. Just as observing that this or that volume of water is boiling at 100°C, at the pressure which obtains near the surface of the earth, gives us evidence for the conclusion that if a given unobserved volume of water were to be heated to that temperature at that pressure, then it would boil; so, too, given the basic soundness of the IOT, the similar pro (or con) attitudes of qualified human judges toward X give us evidence for the conclusion that if there were an IO, then he, too, would have pro (or con) attitudes toward X. (They do not, of course, count as evidence that there is such an IO, any more than our observations of a given volume of water being heated to 100°C at pressure P by themselves give us evidence that there are other, unobserved volumes of water.)

However, since, as I have said, there are sometimes conflicting attitudes among qualified human moral judges, the question arises as to why *these* attitudes don't give us evidence that some IO's would have a pro-attitude toward X and that some would have a con-attitude and, perhaps, that some would be indifferent. But now, if they are sound, the arguments of Chapter 1 establish the existence of a supremely perfect being; and I submit that the concept of a supremely perfect being is such that being supremely perfect is broadly logically necessary and sufficient for being the source of morality. This consideration is supported by the fact that billions of theists believe that the concept of God is the concept of an ultimate ground of the truth and falsity of our moral judgments. Now we have seen that the arguments of Chapter 1, if sound, establish, not only the existence of a supremely perfect being, but his essential uniqueness: there cannot be more than one of him. Moreover, ambivalence toward X would be a defect in a supremely perfect being. Anything, with respect to which he has a pro or con attitude is such that either he has a pro-attitude toward it or he has a con-attitude toward it, but not both. It follows that, if the arguments of Chapter 1 are sound, then there is a single IO, whose pro or con attitudes toward X are canonical, and, hence, that the nonsemantical IO theorist need not be committed to the unpalatable thesis that the massive bombing of civilian populations is sometimes both morally good and morally bad and neither.

It is of note that, barring the present version of the IO theory, the IO theorist has no reason to maintain that, when a conflict of attitudes of the contemplated kind occurs, we can avoid relativism by the simple expedient of claiming that people with such and such an attitude are always better qualified moral judges than are people with a conflicting attitude. For, barring the present version of the IO theory, the IO theorist could not explain why there should not be different *ideal observers* with corresponding conflicting attitudes.

It is clear that the envisaged theory has to be a nonsemantical theory, since intelligent atheists are perfectly capable of making valid moral judgments. In 5.10 I shall offer a definition of 'morally good' and 'morally bad' which is compatible with the latter fact.

5.7 I do not want to maintain that God's pro and con attitudes are essentially involved in *non*moral values. However, a nonsupernaturalist Ideal Observer Theory is the best account of many judgments about nonmoral value. Thus, '1984 was a very good year for this wine' makes tacit reference, not to a supremely perfect ideal observer, but to human connoisseurs. Moreover, some judgments of nonmoral value are merely expressive of the attitudes of the speaker, for example, 'That was a terrible dinner'. But moral and nonmoral value have in common that they are based on *someone's* pro and con attitudes.

5.8 But what about the judgment that there is a supremely knowledgeable and powerful being (namely, God) who is supremely morally good? Am I not committed to the distressing conclusion that it leads to an unacceptable regress, since God's being supremely morally good, and *a fortiori* morally good, consists in his being favored by another supremely morally good being whose moral goodness consists in *his* being favored by still another supremely morally good being, and so on? The answer is that, as we saw in 1.4, it is not logically possible for there to be more than one supremely morally good being, so that, since God, the one and only supremely morally good being, is demonstrably the ground of moral goodness in others, his own moral goodness must consist in his favoring *himself*. (His *supreme* moral goodness must consist in its being logically impossible for him to favor any other being to nearly as great an extent as he favors himself.)

A related objection to my version of the IOT is that if a person, S, is *impartial* with respect to X iff S bases his attitude toward X on facts which are such that an Ideal Observer favors S's basing his attitude toward X on those facts, then we are confronted with an unacceptable regress of impartial Ideal Observers. The answer is simply that (a) it is logically impossible for there to be more than one (supremely perfect) Ideal Observer and (b) since the impartiality of his human creatures consists in his favoring *them* because they base their pro and con attitudes on such and such facts, *his* impartiality consists in his favoring *himself* for doing the same.

5.9    A standard objection to ethical supernaturalism is that God would not have a good reason for having the pro and con attitudes, which in fact he has, and, hence, that they would be merely arbitrary. But this is puzzling. For surely it is not a defect in *human* moral judges that we have (1) a con-attitude toward inflicting unwanted torture and death on someone solely for the purpose of getting sexual gratification and (2) a pro-attitude toward a person's frustrating some significant, innocent desire of his solely in order to benefit another person, even though we cannot construct a sound argument which would make us more justified in having those attitudes than we would be if we knew of no such argument. (Atheists are no less justified in having those attitudes than are theists.)

*Some* human pro and con attitudes *can*, of course, be justified. The following is a justification for having a con-attitude toward Jones's action at time T: 'It was an instance of inflicting unwanted pain and death solely for the purpose of getting sexual pleasure.' And the following is a justification for having a pro-attitude towards the action which Smith performed at time T: 'It was an instance of a person's frustrating a harmless desire of his in order to benefit another person.' But there is surely no reason to believe that the pro and con attitudes of God toward specific actions on specific occasions cannot be similarly justified.

5.10    Finally the reader may be skeptical about my claim to be advancing a nonsemantical theory of 'morally good' and 'morally bad' in the absence of a plausible *definition* of those terms. But such a definition is, in fact, available: 'X is morally bad' means 'X possesses a property in virtue of which 'morally bad' is true of it'; and 'X is morally good' means 'X possesses a property in virtue of which 'morally good' is true of it.' Needless to say, if this kind of definition of a term were generally adequate, then dictionaries would be irrelevant. But I submit that this kind of definition is the best that we can do *with respect just to 'morally good' and 'morally bad'*, since if I am right about the nature of moral goodness and badness, many people, especially many philosophers, are mistaken about it, and I need some way of calling their attention to the properties which I am theorizing about. Of course, prescientific people did not, and do not, know that, say, water is $H_2O$; and yet we can do better, by way of calling their attention to what the chemist is theorizing about, than simply to say 'It is what the term 'water' is true of'. But that is because water has phenomenal properties, and, hence, we can literally point to it. But, if I am right about the nature of moral goodness and badness, we cannot literally point to them, since we cannot literally point to God. However, if someone wants to maintain that the contemplated way of calling attention to what I am theorizing about (namely, the nature of moral goodness and badness) does not count as a *definition*, strictly speaking, I am not strongly averse to obliging her by maintaining (with G. E. Moore) that 'morally good' and 'morally bad' are indefinable. The important thing here is, not whether I am using the word 'definition' correctly, but whether I have successfully called attention to the *subject matter* which I have been *theorizing* about.

# 6

# How to Apply the Ideal Observer Theory: The Controversy over Artificial Contraception and Abortion

---

6.1   As we have seen in the last two chapters, theists are right in thinking that God grounds morality. Moreover, as we saw in the last chapter, they are correct in believing that the intuitions of reflective and impartial human moral judges are, for the most part, trustworthy. But I submit that this latter view can, paradoxically, be used to undermine some widespread contemporary theistic beliefs about precisely what it is that God favors and disfavors. The alleged wrongness of artificial contraception and abortion are cases in point.

6.2   As is well known, conservative Roman Catholics, including the Pope and the Curia, hold that, though it is morally admissible to *omit* to have sex for the purpose of avoiding pregnancy, it is always wrong to *commit* the act of preventing pregnancy via artificial contraception (henceforth, 'contraception,' for simplicity). Let us look, then, at some cases in which the omission–commission distinction is intuitively morally relevant.

   Consider a case in which I am told by a band of sadistic brigands that unless I shoot and kill a given individual, A, then *they* will shoot and kill him. It is intuitive that, in this case, my omitting to save A is preferable to my committing the act of shooting A. But I submit that the explanation may well be that I would be doing more violence to my conception of myself, were I to engage in the act of shooting and killing someone than were I to do nothing at all. After all, the world is full of dying people whom I must regularly omit to save; but it is not full of people whom I regularly kill. And, if it were, then I would be a very different sort of person from the sort of person I want to be.

However, it is surely nowadays false that most people who use contraceptives are doing violence to their conception of themselves. And if the conservative claims here that they *should* be so doing, since using contraception is a *commission*, rather than an omission, he can be met with the rejoinder that not all (or even many) commissions are immoral (for example, my committing the act of closing the window), and so we need a much better explanation of why contraception is seriously wrong.

Similar considerations apply to the case in which the brigands will kill not A, but another person, B, unless I shoot A. Again, it is intuitively better that I omit to save B than that I kill A. But the explanation may well be, once again, that I would be doing violence to my conception of myself, were I to do the latter, rather than the former. This can be confirmed by the consideration that it is intuitive that it *would* be better for me to shoot and kill A if *thousands* of people, including A, would be killed by the brigands, were I to omit to kill A. In that *case*, my omitting to save thousands would also be an instance of my doing violence to my conception of myself.

A similar case, cited by Gilbert Harman,[1] is one in which a doctor cuts up one of his patients in order to obtain organs for five patients who will otherwise die. Clearly his omitting to save the five patients is intuitively morally preferable to his committing the act of killing and cutting up the other patient. But it becomes more and more difficult to believe that the doctor would be doing something wrong by killing and cutting up one patient in order to save the lives of others, as the *number* of the latter increases (say, to one million). And I submit that this can be explained in terms of the doctor's having a right not to do violence to his conception of himself by omitting to save a million people. But *is* the fact that the doctor would be doing violence to his conception of himself by killing and cutting up one patient in order to save *five* others, all that is intuitively relevant here? I think that many reflective people will think that it is not. I shall return to a discussion of this case in 6.13.

6.3   The so-called Doctrine of Double Effect is frequently claimed by conservative Roman Catholics to be a very intuitive doctrine, and one which essentially involves the moral relevance of the omission–commission distinction. Thus, it is said by proponents of the Doctrine of Double Effect that if an action is performed with a highly valuable consequence in view, and that action has as a foreseen consequence a second effect, namely, the death of some innocent people, the action may nonetheless be justified. An example of this is the strategic bomber who, in a just war, drops bombs on an ammunition factory, with the foreseen consequence that some innocent civilians who are in the vicinity will die. Since the conservative Catholic holds that it is always wrong to *commit* the act of killing innocent persons, he concludes that the strategic bomber simply *omits* to save the lives of the innocent civilians in the vicinity.

I shall subsequently argue that even given (what can be doubted) that the strategic bomber case, and other such cases, essentially involve an *omission* to save, what is really morally relevant in such cases is the satisfaction of a condition which the rhythm method does not satisfy.

But at present I want to set out a different criticism. Even given that the contemplated strategic bomber is simply omitting to save the innocent civilians, we have a moral issue on our hands here because his behavior has the foreseen consequence that some innocent civilians will die; and it is *normally* wrong to behave in that way.

It follows that, if he wishes to fall back on the Doctrine of Double Effect, the conservative needs to tell us (a) who, exactly, is harmed by the use of contraceptives and (b) whose life we are justifiably omitting to prolong by omitting to copulate during a woman's fertile period. Is it the gamete pair? Is the gamete pair a person to whom we have a moral obligation not to destroy it, but no obligation to save it, that is, to see to it that it forms a zygote? Here the conservative may say that the use of the rhythm method is *not* a case of omitting to save the gamete pair, since, in the absence of sexual intercourse, there *is* no such entity. But, in the case of a woman with a highly predictable fertile period and a male with a high sperm count, we can know that *if* they had copulated during the woman's fertile period, then pregnancy *would* have resulted. That is to say, we can know that a sperm and an egg, which *would* have united to form a zygote, is being prevented from doing so (though, of course, we cannot specify precisely *which* sperm and egg would have formed the zygote).

6.4   At this point the conservative may wish to fall back on the following 'slippery-slope' argument. 'Infanticide is intuitively seriously wrong. But it is also intuitive that there is no morally relevant difference between the neonate and the fetus just before it emerges from the womb. And so, too, for any stage of the developing fetus and the immediately preceding stage, until we slide all the way back to the gamete pair. So it is, after all, plausible that we have moral obligations to the gamete pair.'

It is, of course, the case that *some* conservatives will not accept this argument on the ground that the gamete pair does not yet contain DNA molecules. But they are ill-advised not to do so for DNA molecules *per se* make no moral demands on us. Otherwise it would be wrong to brush one's teeth or wash one's face, thereby killing some DNA-inhabited cells. The DNA molecules which are contained in the zygote are different from those which are contained in one's teeth and face, since the former, but not the latter, will, in the normal course of events, become a human person. But this is true as well for the gamete pair.

It may well look as though this argument 'proves' too much, namely, that not only do we have a moral obligation not to destroy the gamete pair by the use of contraceptives, but a moral obligation to *save* it by copulating, when we can predict that it will perish if we fail to have sex at a given time: after all, there are *many* cases in which our obligation to save is intuitively as great, or almost as great, as our obligation not to kill. If, while on a walk, I come upon an infant who is drowning in a shallow pond, my obligation to save her (at the expense only of getting my feet wet) is intuitively as great, or almost as great, as my obligation not to hasten her death by holding her head under water. But let us put off discussing this objection until later. I think it can be met, though not in a way which the conservative can accept. In the meantime, the envisaged slippery slope argument needs further discussion.

6.5   One response to it is, in effect, given by Michael Tooley,[2] who denies that we have a moral obligation not to kill neonates. In the course of his arguments, Tooley considers a number of examples and counter-examples, some of which make reference to Frankensteinian monsters and to kittens with a potentiality for developing into beings with a complex, normal human consciousness. These tend, I think, to muddy our intuitions, and I have replaced them with less bizarre examples of a biologically normal adult human being who has been in a coma all her life and of severely retarded human infants. These new examples have the virtue of being better clarifiers of our intuitions, while not distorting the main thrust of Tooley's argument.

Tooley maintains, correctly, I think, that we can wrongfully harm a being only if we deprive him of something which he desired in the past or desires now or will desire in the future. Let us look first at what Tooley says about future desires. Suppose that some music-lovers painlessly castrate a boy soprano who has not in the past, and does not now, desire not to be castrated, but who, in the normal course of events, *will* come to desire sexual maturity. Because he will exist at a future time when that desire will be frustrated, the music-lovers seriously wrong him in present time. Moreover, consider the case of a female child whom her parents condition in such a way, while she is growing up, that she does not come to desire, as a biological adult, to be more than a passive helpmate. Then, even though her parents' treatment of her does not result in a future frustrated desire, as in the case of the boy soprano, they have none the less wronged her because she will exist at a future time when she *would* have desired to be a fully fledged adult person, had they not brought her up to be simply a homemaker.

But now suppose that the boy soprano does not satisfy what I shall call 'Tooley's future-existence clause': suppose instead that he is dying of an incurable disease which will take his life before he would have come to desire sexual maturity. Then the music-lovers do not wrong him by castrating him in present time. And so, too, for the female child. If she will die as a child, then it is false that she will become an adult and *a fortiori* false that she would have had such and such adult desires. So her parents do not wrong her by treating her in the envisaged manner. But now infants, who are too young to have a concept of themselves as entities that continue over time, *do* not desire continued existence and, if we kill them, *will* not have such a desire. Hence, they do not satisfy Tooley's future-desire clause and so, according to Tooley, infanticide is morally justified.

But, of course, things are not so simple. And Tooley recognizes this, though not to an adequate extent. He asks us at this point to consider a case of a suicidally depressed patient who requests that his psychiatrist kill him, even though his psychiatrist is convinced, for good reason, that this patient will eventually recover and once again desire continued life. Plainly, it would be seriously wrong for the psychiatrist to acquiesce here, though it is also clear that, if he did, then the contemplated patient would, like a dead infant, not satisfy the future-desire clause. But Tooley thinks that he can successfully deal with this example by maintaining that the suicidally depressed patient differs in a morally relevant way from the neonate in that he *has* desired continued life in the past, that is, Tooley adds to his (present) and future desire clause what I shall call 'a past-desire clause'. And he claims that it is crucial that, while the suicidally depressed patient satisfies it, the infant does not.

6.6  Is Tooley justified in adding the past-desire clause? Perhaps he thinks so because he believes (1) that the case of the dying boy soprano justifies the future-desire clause and (2) that it would, none the less, be wrong to castrate him in present time if, even though he *will* not desire sexual maturity in the future if we castrate him now, he has in the past desired sexual maturity (or, at any rate, has desired not to be castrated). Now, I submit that it is far from clear that *that* particular past-desire clause is *relevant* here, that is, that we *would* be obliged to honor *that* past desire in the case now before us. But, even if we set that consideration aside, Tooley's position is hard to accept. Suppose that Jones has had a strong desire all his life not to be killed, but of late has become permanently comatose, without the slightest chance of recovering from that condition. Would it really be wrong to (painlessly) kill him because of his comatose condition, even though he has had a prior desire for life?

But, for those who are morally opposed even to killing permanently comatose people, there is another objection. Even if having had a prior desire not to be killed is a morally sufficient condition for not killing an individual (for example, the suicidally depressed patient) in present time, it is surely not a *necessary* condition. Consider the case of a woman who has been in a deep coma all her life, and hence has never desired not to be killed, but about whom we know that she will, if we do not kill her, become conscious, and desire not to be killed, in a few minutes. Surely the mere fact that she has never desired not to be killed in the past would not justify our killing her just before she awakens from her coma.

But now what about Tooley's argument for his crucial *future*-desire clause? Isn't he clearly right that, if the boy soprano will die before he can desire sexual maturity, then we are justified in painlessly castrating him in present time? The answer is that it is plainly true that we are so justified, if his death will result from a fatal disease over which we have no control. But suppose that he will not be alive in the future because *we deliberately* bring about his death now. Then Tooley would simply be begging the question on behalf of infanticide were he to maintain that, even under those circumstances, castrating the boy soprano and then killing him would not, in its entirety, be wrong.

6.7 There is still another of Tooley's arguments which we need to examine. It goes roughly as follows:

> Suppose that we are scientists who discover a drug which, when given to a severely retarded human infant, will bring it about that it will, in the near future, develop into a being who desires continued life. And suppose that we inject one of two severely retarded human infants with this drug, but fail to give it to the second one. Surely we are morally justified in omitting to give the second infant the drug and, hence, *would* have been justified in failing to give the drug to the first infant. But if we would have been so justified, then we would *also* be justified in giving a *neutralizing*-agent to the first unwanted infant after we injected it with the drug. And there is no morally relevant difference between thus neutralizing the first infant and painlessly killing it. Hence, we are morally justified in painlessly killing unwanted infants who do not *require* a drug in order to develop a desire for continuing life.

What shall we think of this argument? Some may wish to maintain here that there is normally a morally relevant difference between omission and commission and, hence, that it does not follow just from the fact that it is admissible to *omit* to give the second infant the drug that it is also admissible to give the first infant a neutralizer. And others may wish to claim that there is a morally relevant difference between neutralizing the first infant and killing it. But, though, as we have seen, there is sometimes a morally relevant difference between omission and commission, I doubt that it obtains here. And I shall not pursue the question of whether killing is worse than neutralizing in the contemplated case. Rather, I shall say a few words about whether in fact we would be within our moral rights in failing to give the drug to either infant (plainly, if it is all right to fail to inject the one, it is all right to fail to inject both), and then I shall proceed to come more directly to grips with Tooley's argument.

Would it be all right to fail to give the drug in the first place? Suppose, to begin with, that it is scarce. Then giving it to just this or that particular infant would not, I think, be morally required but, *pace* Tooley, it is *not* clear that we would be morally justified in not giving it to any severely retarded human infant at all. But set that consideration aside, and suppose that the drug is as plentiful as say, water. Then there will be no nonarbitrary and nonpreposterous answer to the question 'How many severely retarded infants must we inject with the drug?' For example, 'Just eight' will be arbitrary, and 'All the severely retarded infants there are' will be preposterous: surely we would not have a moral obligation to render ourselves destitute by spending all of our waking hours injecting severely retarded infants. So, in case the drug is very *plentiful*, it would be morally admissible not to give it to anyone.

But nothing of interest follows from that. For things are quite different once we *have* administered the drug. Though it may have been morally admissible *not* to have given the drug to the first infant in the first place, it simply does not follow that, having once injected the first infant, it is morally all right to give it the neutralizer and/or to kill it. For it surely does not follow from the fact that it *would* have been all right for me *not* to marry a woman in the first place that, *once I have done so*, it is morally admissible for me to be a philanderer, nor does it follow from the fact that I would have justifiably failed to promise to meet you in my office at 5 p.m. that it is acceptable to *break* that promise *once I have made it*. And so Tooley needs to tell us (but does not) why things should be otherwise, once in fact we have given the drug to the contemplated infant.

It follows that Tooley's second defense of infanticide is as defective as his first one.

6.8   It is doubtful, then, that the slippery-slope argument can be faulted on the ground that it is morally admissible to kill neonates. But now consider the following parody of the slippery-slope argument: 'It is intuitive that we have no moral obligations to the gamete pair. But there is intuitively no morally relevant difference between the gamete pair and the zygote which the former would have become. And it is intuitive that there would have been no morally relevant difference between the zygote at moment, M, and the developing organism a moment later; and so on until we reach the infant who does not yet desire continued life and who would have existed had the gamete pair formed a zygote. Hence, there is after all nothing wrong with killing neonates.'

It is clear, I think, that this argument is fallacious. At any rate, the conservative will surely think so. But I submit that the best explanation of what is wrong with it undermines the conservative's position on abortion. One attempt to explain its wrongness is as follows: 'A similar argument is that there is no difference between an acorn and an oak tree, since if we start with the acorn at moment, M, and then consider the developing tree a moment later, we will find an insignificantly small difference; and so on for any two successive moments as we trace the development of the oak tree. This argument is plainly fallacious, in view of the fact that the *sum* of very small differences can be a very *large* difference. And a similar consideration applies to the envisaged parody.' But this explanation is, at best, incomplete, since the slippery-slope argument and its parody are not concerned just with small *physical* differences but with small physical differences which make a *morally relevant* difference.

Evidently, the best explanation of what is wrong with the contemplated parody needs to be expanded as follows: 'The *sum* of small *morally relevant* differences can be a very *large* morally relevant difference. And large *physical* differences can make a large *morally* relevant difference. Thus, the large *physical* difference between the gamete pair and the neonate makes a large *morally relevant* difference between the former and the latter. And the best way of understanding *this* is to conclude that as we move up the envisaged slope from the gamete pair to the neonate, the *prima facie* obligation not to kill the developing organism at that point on the slope becomes less and less easily overridden by such considerations as the mother's health, the genetic defectiveness of the fetus, the poverty into which it will be born, and so on. But this entails that, as we move *down* the slope, the *prima facie* obligation not to kill the developing organism becomes more and more easily overridden by those considerations. It follows that the conservative's absolutist prohibition against abortion is mistaken, or, at any rate, that there is no sound slippery-slope argument which will support it.'

6.9 But why should it be the case that the less developed the organism the less stringent the *prima facie* obligation not to kill it? The basis for an answer to this question has been laid in 1.5. It will be recalled that I argued there that the concept of a supremely perfect being entails having a higher degree of existence than any other individual, and since I argued in Chapter 2 that such a being exists, I argued in effect on behalf of there being degrees of existence.

The reader will recall that I used as an example the contrast between the completed statue and the partially completed statue, and pointed out that the former has a higher degree of existence than does the latter. Now degrees of existence are the same as degrees of identity. The more the partially completed statue physically resembles the completed statue, the more identical with the latter it becomes, that is, the more fully it exists.

I submit that this consideration enables us to understand why there should be different degrees of stringency of our *prima facie* obligation not to kill the developing embryo and fetus: the more the fetus physically resembles an infant who has a concept of herself and a desire that that self continue to exist, the more identical with the latter does the former become, and, hence, since rights are obviously in some sense based on desires (Tooley is right about that), the more of a right to life does that fetus possess, that is, the more *prima facie* wrong it becomes to destroy it.

6.10   There are two objections to this explanation which we need to consider here.

(1)   'Call the life-desiring infant 'A' and the developing fetus 'B.' Dore has said in effect that, at a given moment, M, B can be partly identical with A, even if, because B is destroyed at M, A does not exist *after* M. Hence, Dore is committed to the absurd conclusion that B can be partly identical with a nonexistent thing; namely, A.' My reply is that in fact A *does* exist in the envisaged case, but *only partially*. But, for the benefit of doubters, I can dispense with that reply as follows. Consider the case in which A does fully exist after M. An unsuccessful attempt at M to kill B, which is partly identical with (fully existent) A, would normally be to some extent morally wrong, because it would be an attempt to kill A, which, since B is partly identical with A at M, partially exists at M. And it follows that a *successful* attempt to kill B, which *would* have been partly identical with A, had the attempt been unsuccessful, would also normally be to some extent morally wrong. For a mere lack of success cannot amount to a morally relevant difference.

(2)   'It is normally not as wrong to destroy the partially completed statue as it is to destroy the completed statue. So why

should it be less wrong to destroy B than it is to destroy A?' My answer is that, if we destroy the partially completed statue, we may be frustrating the desires of the sculptor and her admirers to as great an extent as would be the case were we to destroy the completed statue. But, of course, the completed statue will not have a concept of itself and *a fortiori* it will not *itself* desire its continued existence. However, *ex hypothesis* A will have a concept of itself and will desire its continued existence. So even if we would frustrate the desires of other people by killing B to as great an extent as we would frustrate the desires of the sculptor and her admirers by destroying the partially completed statue, it remains true that we would do something even worse by killing B.

6.11  The claim that there are degrees of identity-cum-existence will no doubt be met with skepticism by some philosophers. Suppose that the conservative numbers among them. Then he will want to argue as follows: 'It is far less intuitive that we have no moral obligations with respect to the gamete pair than that my slippery slope argument is fallacious. So I stand by it. And I continue to insist that the Doctrine of Double Effect reinforces that stand.' We need, then, to discuss the Doctrine of Double Effect at still greater length.

Consider the following examples of double effect: A doctor operates on a woman with a cancerous uterus with the foreseen consequence that a highly developed fetus, who would not have died anyway if the operation had not been performed, will in fact die. A strategic bomber drops bombs on an ammunition factory with the foreseen consequence that some innocent civilians who are in the vicinity will die. An engineer on a train, in order to avoid killing five people on the track straight ahead, steers on to a side track with the foreseen consequence that a single individual who is standing there will die.

It looks as if, in all of these cases, the following condition (call it 'C') is satisfied: An individual performs an action for the purpose of bringing about a highly valuable state of affairs, S, and which has the foreseen consequence that someone will be harmed, but *would* have performed that action, and with the same motive, even if her action would not have had that consequence. And it also looks as if satisfying condition C exempts a person from moral blameworthiness, in that her *motive*, in acting as she did, was not to bring about that consequence, but, rather, to bring about S. (Perhaps it should be added here that she is *totally* blameless only if she desires the absence of that consequence.)

But now if the satisfaction of condition C is, indeed, what is morally relevant in cases of double effect, then the use of the rhythm method cannot be justified by reference to the Doctrine of Double Effect. For it is plainly false that the couple who deliberately omits to get pregnant during a woman's fertile periods, would have copulated, and with the same motive, even if they *would* get pregnant at those times. For couples who practice the rhythm method, avoiding pregnancy is *not* an undesired side-effect.

6.12   Let us return to the case which we considered in 6.2, in which a doctor cuts up one of his patients in order to obtain organs which will save the lives of five other patients. Here the following objection may be raised: 'The doctor's motive in cutting up his patient may not have been to harm the patient but just to save five other patients. And if that were so, then he would be as blameless as, say, the strategic bomber who is not motivated to kill the innocent civilians in the vicinity of the ammunition factory.'

The answer is that it is surely intuitive that, though the strategic bomber can justify his action by saying that the death of the innocent civilians was an unwanted side-effect, Harman's doctor cannot justify his action by saying that the death of his patient was an unwanted side-effect. But for convenience, I shall postpone explaining this intuition until 6.13.

Another objection to the thesis that cases of double effect are instances of the satisfaction of condition C is as follows: Philippa Foot discusses a case in which three patients, who cannot be moved, need an emergency operation in order to remain alive, but in which, because of a malfunction in the operating equipment, performing the operation will leak deadly gas into an adjoining room, killing its lone inhabitant – a person who is recovering well and will soon be released from hospital. Foot maintains that it is intuitive that it would be wrong for the envisaged doctor to perform the operation, and explains this intuition in terms of a negative duty on the part of the doctor not to kill the patient in the adjoining room rather than a positive duty to save the three patients.[3] Foot is clearly right here, and it follows that the satisfaction of condition C, in cases involving omission and commission is not sufficient for blamelessness. For the doctor's performing the contemplated operation would satisfy condition C: the doctor would have performed it, and with the same motive, even if the gas were not going to leak or if there had been no one in the adjoining room.

However, I think that what we have here is merely a *utilitarian constraint* on the satisfaction of condition C. I submit that, if we think of a case which is very similar to Foot's, except that the setting is a two-room house on a desert island, our intuitions will tell us that performing the operation in *that* setting would not in fact be morally wrong (so long as it is certain that three people will be saved and that the one in the adjoining room will die). Why should this be?

Let us return to the case of Harman's doctor, who cuts up one of his patients in order to save the lives of five others. This case is, in all essential respects, similar to Foot's hospital case. I said in 6.2 about the former case that it is counter-intuitive that all that is wrong with that doctor is that he would be doing violence to his conception of himself were he to behave in the envisaged manner. And it should be added here that, even if we think of him as *not* doing violence to his self-image, it is counter-intuitive that what he would be doing is morally acceptable. But I submit that our relevant intuitions are affected by the fact that we are considering a *doctor* and that (1) the social institutions in which doctors ordinarily function are such that the practice of committing acts which have the death of a patient as a foreseen outcome are, on the whole, such that if they were permitted, then patients would be worse, rather than better off, and (2) patients will be better, rather than worse off, if doctors *routinely* refrain from committing such acts within the social contexts in which they normally function. But, again, I submit that desert island scenarios lead to different intuitions. And I also submit that the fact that we tend to overlook such scenarios explains our (proper) disinclination to accept the claim that Harman's case can be explained simply in terms of the doctor's doing violence to his self-image. And exactly similar considerations apply to Foot's case: there are rule-utilitarian constraints on the satisfaction of C in those cases.

But this should come as no surprise. Not only is the satisfaction of C not always sufficient for blamelessness, we have seen in effect that it is not always *necessary*. Harman's doctor would surely be blameless were he to cut up one patient in order to save the lives of millions: once again, there are utilitarian constraints on the satisfaction of C.

Still, I submit that the satisfaction of C, even when qualified in terms of utilitarian constraints can give the conservative no cause for rejoicing. For the conservative will surely be hard pressed to explain why it should be true that omitting to copulate during a woman's fertile period can be given a utilitarian justification, even though using contraceptives cannot be adequately justified by utilitarian considerations. Once again, there is nothing wrong with commissions *per se*.

6.13    Let us return to the claim that Harman's doctor, who desires to cut up his patient in order to save five others, could be justified in cutting up his patient by his not desiring to harm her. This is similar to the claim that a person might desire to take a brisk walk at time, t, without desiring to move her legs at t, or, if she can walk on her hands, her arms, or to the claim that a person might desire to swim at time, t, without desiring that her body be partially immersed in a liquid at time t. If someone, S, desires something, x, and the claim that x occurs analytically entails that y occurs, then it is (logically) impossible for S to desire x while not desiring y.

Here it may be objected that Harman's doctor's cutting up his patient and removing her organs, does not *logically* necessitate her being harmed. But I submit that the concept of harm and the concept of an intact body, with all of its organs properly functioning, are such that, with a qualification to be given in 6.14, it is a conceptual truth that cutting someone up and removing her organs counts as harming her.

By contrast, the reason that the strategic bomber of 6.11 can fail to desire that the innocent civilians in the vicinity will die is that his dropping bombs on the ammunition factory does not logically necessitate the presence of innocent civilians in the vicinity, and *a fortiori* it does not logically necessitate their being killed or even harmed. Moreover, the reason that the engineer, who steers on to the side track, can fail to desire the death of the single individual there is that his steering on to the side track does not logically necessitate the presence of that individual there and *a fortiori* it does not logically necessitate his being killed or harmed. And the reason that the doctor who operates on a cancer patient, with the foreseen consequence that her highly developed fetus will die, can fail to desire the death of that fetus is that operating on that woman does not logically necessitate her pregnancy; since it does not logically necessitate the presence of the fetus in her womb. However, the claim that, since Harman's doctor cutting up his patient does not logically necessitate his harming his patient, because it does not logically necessitate his patient being in the vicinity, is patently absurd.

It looks very much, then, as though the satisfaction of condition C, suitably qualified, is what is essential in cases of double effect. So, since the conservative cannot claim that the rhythm method satisfies condition C *per se*, he must fall back, once again, on utilitarianism. But then it is entirely unclear as to why he should think that utilitarian considerations, though they justify omitting to have sex during a woman's fertile period, do not also justify the use of contraceptives.

6.14  I have said that it is a conceptual truth that cutting someone up and removing her organs normally counts as harming her. The reason for the qualifier, 'normally,' is this: not *all* conceivable cases of cutting up a patient and removing her organs are cases of harm. For example, Harman's doctor would not be harming his patient if she were permanently comatose and, hence, 'better off dead'. But in that case the doctor would not be doing something wrong by cutting up his patient in order to save the lives of five others. And this is perfectly consistent with the truth of C: the doctor's action would not be a violation of it. An analogous case is one in which a doctor removes a permanently comatose patient from a life-support machine. Since the patient is at least as 'well off dead', the doctor does not violate condition C, and this accounts for the fact that even most conservative Catholics intuit that what the doctor does in removing the patient from the life support machine is morally acceptable.

It is of note that there are some bizarre possible worlds in which Harman's doctor would not be doing what is wrong in cutting up his patient, for example, a world in which the patient's body would be miraculously restored a moment later. But, once again, in cutting his patient up in that world, Harman's doctor would not be violating condition C.

6.15  Here someone may ask why we should not dispense with the satisfaction of condition C altogether and make do instead simply with an agent's doing violence to his conception of himself by committing the act of killing or harming someone and/or with the utilitarian constraints of 6.12.

The answer is this: consider the contrast between the terror bomber, whose aim is to demoralize the enemy by killing innocent civilians, and the strategic bomber, whose aim is not to kill the innocent civilians in the area, but to destroy the ammunition factory. Though the strategic bomber satisfies condition C, the terror bomber clearly does not: the claim that he would have killed innocent civilians at time t, even if no innocent civilians would have been within reach of his bombs at time t, is absurd on its face.

But now suppose that the terror bomber and the strategic bomber are (a) equally well-informed about whether their actions at time t will shorten the war and (b) not at all certain that in fact they will do so. I submit that it is intuitive that, under those circumstances (though not under *all* conceivable circumstances) what the terror bomber does is morally worse than what the strategic bomber does. And I submit further that the explanation of this intuition is that, though the terror bomber clearly does not satisfy condition C, the strategic bomber does satisfy it.

However, even if I am wrong about this, the conservative cannot, as we have seen, cite utility as the justification of his claim that, while omitting to get pregnant is morally acceptable, committing the act of preventing pregnancy by the use of contraceptives is not.

6.16    I said in 6.4 that I would return to the case of the drowning infant in the shallow pond. Now it is surely true that I would have a stringent obligation to save her, or, at any rate, that that is the case in the real world. But suppose that everywhere I went, I encountered *thousands* of shallow ponds, each of which was occupied by a drowning infant. And suppose that there is no morally relevant difference between my saving the infant in any given shallow pond, S, and my saving infants in any *other* shallow pond. Then either I would have no obligation to save the infant in S, or I would be obliged to save as many as I could, thereby using all of my time and energy in the saving of drowning infants. But the latter is preposterous. Hence I would have no obligation to save the infant in S. (The real world is very like this imaginary world with respect to starving people.)

An argument on behalf of not saving the gamete pair can be based on this consideration: 'There is no morally relevant difference between my getting a given woman, W, pregnant during her fertile period and my getting any other fertile woman pregnant. Hence, if I were obliged to get W pregnant during her fertile period, I would be obliged to get as many fertile women pregnant as I could. But the latter is absurd. Hence, the conservative who says that I have an obligation to the gamete pair not to destroy it, can, after all, account for the fact that I have no obligation to save it.'

But, of course, he cannot offer this explanation, since he holds that there *is* a morally relevant difference between one's *married* partner and other sexual partners, that is, he holds that sex with the latter though not with the former is sinful.

6.17 The conservative thinks that there is a morally relevant difference between the two following injunctions: (a) 'Don't ever commit the act of trying to prevent pregnancy when having sex,' and (b) 'Don't ever omit to have sex at a given time t, in order to avoid pregnancy.' One wonders what the conservative would say about a devout person who, say, prays during intercourse that pregnancy will not result. But set that aside. It may be that the conservative thinks that the distinction between these two injunctions is like the distinction that a doctor, who in dealing with a heart patient, would draw between (c) 'Don't ever, when walking, try to avoid exerting yourself' and (d) 'Never at any time, t, avoid walking in order to avoid exerting yourself.'

But the analogy breaks down. For the point of injunction (c) would be to advise the patient to exert herself sometimes, since that will be good for her, that is, the following is absurd, 'Don't, ever, when going for a walk, try to avoid exerting yourself; but it's perfectly all right never to go for a walk.' However, the conservative, who admires celibacy, *a fortiori* holds that it is perfectly all right never to have sex with anyone. So he is committed to this advice: 'Never, when having sex, try to prevent pregnancy, but it's perfectly all right never to have sex.' And that certainly looks very much like 'Always, when walking, exert yourself, but it's perfectly all right never to go for a walk in order to avoid exerting yourself.'

6.18 The conservative frequently maintains that the use of contraceptives is 'unnatural' and, hence, immoral. Let us suppose that he does not simply *mean* by 'unnatural,' immoral, that is that he is not simply arguing that contraception is immoral because it is immoral. Is his position, then, that deliberately interfering with a normal bodily function is always seriously wrong? If so, then he is committed to the absurd conclusion that, say, holding one's breath or repressing a sneeze or keeping one's eyes closed when not drowsy, and so on is always seriously wrong. But if the conservative falls back on the claim that *contraception*, in particular, is seriously wrong, in the sense that God-cum-nature obviously intend sexual intercourse for procreation, then he is being inconsistent both with respect to the rhythm method and with respect to copulation on the part of a married couple, at least one of whom is sterile, for example, a woman after menopause.

It is, of course, open to the conservative to opt for consistency by denying that the rhythm method and sterile sex are morally admissible. But the very fact that he does not do so is an indication of how draconian a stand that would be.

# 7
# Causal Realism and the Egocentric Predicament

7.1    It is my contention that a justified theory of how God grounds the physical universe must be based on a discussion of the nature of our knowledge of the physical universe. In this chapter and part of the next, I shall argue that a version of phenomenalism constitutes the best account of that knowledge; and then I shall conclude Chapter 8 with a defense of the thesis that God provides the ultimate explanation of the truth of a phenomenalist explanation of what physical things consist of.

7.2    It is currently fashionable to hold that a person cannot, and need not, base inferences to physical objects in her immediate environment on any of her mental states. But there is an argument to the contrary. It needs to be prefaced by an argument that perceiving physical objects essentially involves seeming to perceive them and a rather lengthy defense of that argument. For simplicity, I shall talk about seeing and seeming to see, but what I shall say about these can, I submit, be seen upon reflection to be applicable to other modes of perception.

    The argument that I have in mind (call it 'G') runs as follows:

(1)    Imagine a case in which (a) someone, Z, sees a puddle of blood on his living-room rug; (b) Z has reason to believe that he does not see blood on the rug; (c) Z says, 'I seem to see blood on the rug'.

(2)    The fact that Z really does see blood on the rug (though he does not know it) does not make Z mistaken in saying, 'I seem to see blood on the rug'. Z's utterance makes a true statement, therefore. It follows that Z is in a certain state in virtue of which

what he says is true, as well as being in a state, in virtue of which it is true that he sees blood on the rug.

(3) But it is impossible to understand what difference between the case under discussion and any other conceivable instance of Z's seeing anything would be marked by saying that some instance of Z's seeing an object is not an instance in which the state affirmed by 'I seem to see. . .' is present. (We can, of course, conceive of a case which differs from the envisaged case in that Z does not seem to see the very same object which he sees. Thus Z might seem to see a rat, whereas what he truly sees is an old shoe. However, we cannot conceive of a case which differs from the envisaged case in that Z sees some object at a certain place but fails to seem to see any object of any sort at that place.)

(4) It follows that 'I seem to see. . .' affirms the existence of a state which one must, logically, be in if he is to see anything. But 'I seem to see. . .' does not mean the same as 'I see. . .,' and, hence, it does not affirm the existence of precisely the same state as is affirmed to exist by 'I see. . . .' This may be expressed by saying that what 'I seem to see. . .' affirms is only a logically necessary, not a sufficient, condition of what 'I see. . .' affirms.

So much for the exposition of G. Let us turn now to a discussion of some criticisms of it.

7.3  Back in the days when sense-datum theory was frequently discussed, Gilbert Ryle wrote of sentences of the same sort as 'I seem to see. . .' that they are used for the purpose of making 'guarded statements of what I am tempted or inclined to judge to be the case'.[1] And G. J. Warnock said that 'the essential function of the language of 'seeming' is that it is noncommittal as to the actual facts'.[2] One plausible interpretation of these remarks is as follows. The role of 'seems', on all occasions of its use, is exactly comparable to the role of 'maybe': both words, whenever they are uttered, are used solely for the purpose of asserting a proposition in a guarded or tentative manner or of indicating a noncommittal attitude toward that proposition.[3]

A criticism of G emerges from this analysis of 'I seem to see. . . .' In step 2 of G it is said that Z's utterance makes a true statement. But, given the similarity of 'seem' to 'maybe,' this will not do.

Guarded or noncommittal expressions such as Z's cannot be used to make false statements, and, therefore, they cannot be used to make true ones. The point may be illustrated by considering a sentence containing 'maybe'– for example, 'Maybe it will rain today'. What is said by this sentence is compatible both with its raining today and with its not raining today, and, hence, there is no conceivable state of affairs which can falsify it.[4] But, then, since what is said by 'Maybe it will rain today' cannot be false, it cannot be true either. For what cannot be false can be true only if it is a necessarily true proposition such as that expressed by '2+2=4'. And it can hardly be maintained that what is expressed by 'Maybe it will rain today' is such a proposition. Exactly similar considerations apply to Z's utterance. But, now, since Z's utterance does not make a true statement, it must be a mistake to say – as is also said in step 2 – that 'Z is in a certain state in virtue of which what he says is true'.

Step 4 fares no better, in view of the similarity of 'seem' to 'maybe'. It is a gross mistake to claim that 'I seem to see. . .' is used to affirm the existence of a state of the speaker which is logically necessary, but not sufficient, for his seeing some object. This mistake is exactly similar to that which one would be making were one to claim that 'Maybe it will rain today' affirms the existence of something which is logically necessary, but not sufficient, for rain today. The trouble is that 'I seem to see X' does not affirm of the speaker something in any way different from what we affirm of him when we say that he sees X, and hence it does not affirm the existence of something which is only necessary, not sufficient, for his seeing X. Just in case, and to the extent that, 'I seem to see X' is used to affirm anything at all of the speaker, it affirms (in a guarded manner) exactly what he affirms when he says that he sees X.

The criticism of G just presented is based on the claim that 'seems', in all its occurrences (including its occurrences in conjunction with 'see'), behaves like 'maybe.' What may appear to recommend this claim is that, if it were true, then it would be easy to see why 'I seem to see X' is not generally uttered when the speaker has no doubt that he sees X. One does not generally make statements in a guarded manner, nor evince a noncommittal attitude toward propositions, when one is certain of their truth. Moreover, it might appear, at least at first glance, that, unless we adopt the analysis of 'I seem to see X' that is under discussion, we shall not be able to formulate an adequate explanation. But this, as I shall subsequently show, is mere appearance. And, anyway, there are certain considerations which leave us no choice but to repudiate the analysis now in question and, along with it, the criticism of G just considered.

First of all, while it is true that 'I seem to see X' is not generally uttered by a person who firmly believes that he sees X, it is plainly false that it cannot be uttered in perfect propriety by a person who firmly believes that he does not see X but suffers a hallucination instead. And this is sufficient to refute the claim that 'seems,' like 'maybe,' functions in all its occurrences, including its occurrences in connection with forms of the verb 'to see,' as a device for enabling the speaker to make a guarded or tentative statement or to evince a noncommittal attitude toward a proposition. For it is less than completely candid for one to assert a proposition tentatively or to evince a noncommittal attitude toward it when one is convinced that the proposition is false; and perceptual propositions are no exception to this rule. Z cannot say with perfect candor 'Maybe I see blood on the rug' when he firmly believes that he suffers a hallucination. But it would be perfectly proper for him to say 'I seem to see blood on the rug' in those circumstances. It follows that, in case the speaker believes that he hallucinates, 'I seem to see. . .' does not mean the same as 'Maybe I see. . .,' that is, it is not used as a guarded or noncommittal utterance.

Someone may wish to reply that at least the analysis under discussion and the criticism of G which is based on it hold good for the case in which Z is uncertain about whether he sees blood on the rug (rather than convinced that he does). It may be said that in this case, at any rate, Z would simply be asserting in a guarded way that he sees blood on the rug or evincing a noncommittal attitude toward that proposition. But I think that it is dubious that Z would here mean something quite different by 'I seem to see blood on the rug' from what he would mean were he convinced that he suffers a hallucination. Suppose that he starts off in a state of doubt and says, 'I seem to see blood on the rug,' and that he subsequently becomes convinced that he hallucinates and says, 'I still seem to see the blood' . Surely he would not be speaking inappropriately in saying the latter, and yet his use of the word 'still' indicates that the second utterance has the same sense as the first one. Moreover, even if we waive this consideration, the reply in question is certainly not sufficient to sustain the proposed criticism of G. *Qua* attack on G, the reply may be circumvented by the simple expedient of imagining that Z is convinced that he suffers a hallucination. It will not do to answer that in that case 'I seem to see blood' is used by Z to state that he hallucinates, and hence that it is plainly not used to affirm that Z is in a state which is logically necessary for genuine vision. The claim that Z uses 'I seem to see blood' to state that he is suffering a hallucination entails that Z says what is false (since Z does in fact see blood on the rug). And this last thesis is certainly mistaken. Just as one who says 'I seem to see X' does not say something which is falsified by the fact that he suffers a hallucination in which he merely seems to see X, so, too, he does not say something which is falsified by the fact that he does not suffer a hallucination but really sees X instead.

There is another consideration which has a bearing on the present discussion. If it were really the case that 'I seem to see. . .' meant the same as 'Maybe I see. . ,' then the criticism of step 2 of G would be accurate, at least to this extent: there would be no conceivable state of affairs in virtue of which what is said by 'I seem to see. . .' could properly be called false – just as there is no conceivable state of affairs in virtue of which what is said by 'Maybe it will rain today' can properly be called false. But in fact this is not the case. Though what is said by 'I seem to see X' is not incompatible either with the speaker's seeing X or with his suffering a hallucination in which he merely seems to see X, it is incompatible with his having a hallucination in which he seems to see some object other than X. A person who says for example, 'I seem to see a brown horse at place P' when in fact, he suffers a hallucination, in which he seems to see a purple dragon at place P, tells a falsehood. Moreover, what is said by 'I seem to see X at P' is incompatible with the speaker's seeing some object other than X at P which does not look like X to him. Thus, if I see a cat on the mat and it does not look like a dog to me, I tell a falsehood by saying, 'I seem to see a dog on the mat.' Similar considerations do not hold for 'Maybe I see X.' States of affairs which involve the speaker suffering a hallucination in which he seems to see some object other than X do not falsify what he says by this utterance. Though what the speaker seems to see is a purple dragon, he would not be speaking falsely – indeed, it might be that he would not be speaking insincerely – were he to say 'But maybe what I see is, in reality, a brown horse (instead).' Moreover, the state of affairs in which the speaker sees Y and it does not look like Y to him does not falsify (nor necessarily render insincere) what he says when he says, 'Maybe what I see is, in reality, X (which looks like Y).'

The essential point here can be put as follows: if I say, 'I seem to see X at P', and it is later discovered either that I suffered a hallucination in which what I seemed to see at P was not X but Y, or that I really saw Y at P and that it did not look like X to me, then *eo ipso* I am convicted of having said what is false. If, on the other hand, I say, 'Maybe I see X at P', and these same things are later discovered, then I cannot be accused of having said what is false (nor is it necessarily the case that I can even be accused of being misleading). It follows that 'I seem to see. . .' does not mean the same as 'Maybe I see. . .'.

A final word in this connection. I do not wish to deny that a person who says 'I seem to see. . .' may be either asserting in a guarded way that he sees the object which he mentions or evincing a noncommittal attitude toward the proposition that he sees it. All that I have tried to establish here is that this is never all that one does, nor – since 'I seem to see. . .' has basically the same sense when the speaker is in doubt as when he is convinced that he is hallucinating – the primary thing that one does, when one says, 'I seem to see. . .'. If I am right, then the criticism of G which we have been considering is without foundation.

7.4   Another claim about 'I seem to see. . . ,' from which it follows that G is not a sound argument, is that 'I seem to see. . .' has the same meaning as 'I am inclined to believe that I see. . .' . At first glance it may appear that this claim does not really differ from the claim that 'I seem to see. . .' means the same as 'Maybe I see. . .', since it is tempting to suppose that 'I am inclined to believe. . .' plays a role exactly like that of 'maybe'. But it is, I think, difficult to reconcile the thesis that 'I am inclined to believe. . .' has the same use as 'maybe' with the fact that 'He is inclined to believe. . .' and 'You are inclined to believe. . .' are not characteristically guarded or noncommittal expressions. I can say of another person that he is inclined to believe a certain proposition, p, even though I am entirely convinced that p is false (or true). When I say, 'He is (You are) inclined to believe that p', I am not, therefore, asserting p guardedly nor am I evincing a noncommittal attitude toward it. And there is no other proposition which I might be asserting guardedly or toward which I might be evincing a noncommittal attitude. It follows that the expressions in question characteristically affirm something in a nontentative way about the person to whom they refer. And it is difficult to believe that this is not also the case when

'I' is substituted for 'You' and 'He' in these expressions. I take it, therefore, that 'I am inclined to believe that I see. . .' typically makes an unguarded affirmation of the existence of a certain state of the speaker – the state of being inclined to believe that he sees the object which he mentions.

The analysis now under consideration, unlike the Ryle–Warnock analysis, cannot be rejected on the ground that there are no conceivable states of affairs, the existence of which would falsify what is said by 'I am inclined to believe that I see X at place P.' States of affairs in which the speaker is not inclined to believe that he sees X at P but is inclined to believe instead that he sees some object other than X at P – or is not inclined to believe that he sees any object at all occupying P – would falsify what is said by the utterance in question. Moreover, if (as is, perhaps, not obviously wrong) it is possible for a person to be inclined to believe that a certain proposition is true, and, at the same time, to disbelieve that very proposition, then the present analysis of 'I seem to see. . .,' unlike the Ryle–Warnock analysis, is at least not plainly incompatible with the fact that I can say 'I seem to see X' with perfect propriety even though I disbelieve that I see X.

A criticism of G which may be based on the present analysis is as follows. Though step 2 of G is legitimate (it is perfectly correct to say that 'I am inclined to believe that I see blood on the rug' makes a true statement and does so in virtue of a certain state of Z; hence, the same holds true of 'I seem to see blood on the rug'), steps 3 and 4 are plainly false. We can easily conceive of a case which differs from the envisaged case in that, though Z sees some object at P, he is not in the state affirmed by 'I seem to see. . .'. For this is simply to conceive of a case in which Z is not just inclined to believe that he sees some object at P but has no doubt whatever that he does so.

One approach for the philosopher who wishes to defend G against this criticism is to deny that a person can both be inclined to believe that something is the case and, at the same time, convinced that it is not. For, in case this claim is false, then the present analysis of 'I seem to see. . .' is, like the Ryle–Warnock analysis, incompatible with the fact that it is appropriate for a person to say 'I seem to see. . .' when he is convinced that he suffers a hallucination. This much, at least, can be said on behalf of the thesis that disbelieving a proposition is incompatible with being inclined to believe it: a person who told us that he was inclined to believe that some proposition was true when in fact he was convinced that it was false would ordinarily seriously mislead us by so doing. To this it may be replied (a) that, while being inclined to believe p may be incompatible with being fully convinced (firmly believing) that not-p, it is not incompatible with believing not-p with some lesser degree of conviction, and (b) that people who suffer hallucinations are not (and indeed cannot be) fully convinced that they do not see the object which they seem to see. But, while (a) is unexceptionable, (b) appears to be false: it appears that the concepts of hallucination and of being fully convinced of something are not such that it is absurd to say of someone that he is fully convinced that he suffers a hallucination. Indeed, it is true as a matter of fact that hallucinogenic drugs produce hallucinations which the subject knows full well to be hallucinations.

But let us waive this rebuttal (I shall return to it in 6.9). There remain two further arguments against our accepting the analysis of 'I seem to see X' in terms of an inclination on the speaker's part to believe that he sees X.

(1)  We do not ordinarily say 'He seems to see X' or 'You seem to see X' when we are convinced that the person to whom we refer really does see X. Just as a person who says 'I seem to see X' generally indicates that he doubts or disbelieves that he really sees X, so a speaker who utters the second and third-person forms of 'seem to see' generally indicates that he doubts or disbelieves that the person to whom he refers really sees X. But, unfortunately for the proponent of the present analysis, similar considerations do not hold for 'He is inclined to believe that he sees X' and 'You are inclined to believe that you see X'. We frequently say of other people (though not of ourselves) that they are inclined to believe some proposition about the truth of which we, the speakers, have absolutely no doubt.

(2)  I can believe, or be inclined to believe, that what I see is, in reality, an old shoe on my table when it looks to me as though I see (I seem to see) a rat there instead. That is to say, I can believe, or be inclined to believe, that what seems to me to be a rat is in reality an old shoe. I cannot, however, seem to see an old shoe on my table when it looks to me as though I see (I seem to see) a rat there instead. Being inclined to believe that one sees an old shoe cannot, therefore, be the same as seeming to see an old shoe. And, of course, we can generalize: being

inclined to believe that one sees X cannot be the same as seeming to see X.

The present analysis of 'I seem to see. . .', like the Ryle–Warnock analysis, would, if we could accept it, enable us to give an account of the fact that we do not ordinarily say that we seem to see some object when we have no doubt that we do see the object. Whatever may be thought of the claim that a person may be convinced that a certain proposition is false and yet inclined to believe it, it is indisputable that one may not be both convinced that a certain proposition is true and also inclined to believe it. It would plainly be absurd to say, 'I am inclined to believe that I see blood on the rug and I have no doubt at all that I do.' Exactly similar considerations would, of course, be true of seeming to see some object if (as is not the case) this were the same as being inclined to believe that one sees the object.

7.5   Another claim which would, if true, entail that G is unsound and account for the fact that we do not say that we seem to see X when we have do doubt that we see X is the claim that 'I seem to see. . .' means the same as 'I doubt that I see. . .'. If this were so, then (a) 'I seem to see X and I have no doubt that I do' would be self-contradictory, and (b) step 2 of G would be obviously false: since we can easily imagine cases in which a person sees X and does not doubt that he does, we can easily imagine cases in which seeing X is not accompanied by seeming to see. But the present analysis, like the Ryle–Warnock analysis, does not accurately represent the meaning of 'I seem to see. . .' in those cases where the speaker is convinced that he is suffering a hallucination. If he is at all concerned to be accurate, he does not say that he doubts that something is the case when he is convinced that it is not the case. It follows that it is unlikely that the present analysis is an adequate analysis of the meaning of 'I seem to see. . .' on any occasion of its utterance. Moreover, the present analysis can be rejected on the ground that 'He doubts that he sees. . .' and 'You doubt that you see. . .' do not indicate doubt or disbelief on the part of the speaker, while 'He seems to see. . .' and 'You seem to see. . .' do indicate doubt or disbelief. Also, though a person can doubt that he sees Y at P when he seems to see X at P, he cannot seem to see Y at P when he seems to see X at P.

7.6   There is still another claim from which it follows that G is not sound and which would, if true, explain why we do not say 'I seem to see X' when convinced that we do see X. I have in mind the claim that 'I seem to see. . .' means the same as 'I disbelieve that I see. . .'. If this analysis were correct, then, once again, 'I seem to see X and I have no doubt that I see X' would be self-contradictory. Moreover, step 3 of G would be clearly false. But the analysis can be rejected on the ground (a) that it cannot account for the fact that people say 'I seem to see X' when they strongly suspect that they may in reality be seeing X; (b) that 'He disbelieves that he sees X' and 'You disbelieve that you see X' do not indicate that the speaker doubts or disbelieves that the person to whom he refers sees X, while this is not true of 'He seems to see X', and so on; and (c) that a person can disbelieve that he sees Y at P when he seems to see X at P, but he cannot seem to see Y at P when he seems to see X at P.

7.7   At this point, it may appear that I have saved G only at the cost of losing any hope of finding an explanation of the fact that we do not ordinarily say that we seem to see an object unless there is at least some doubt that we do. But in fact a very simple and plausible explanation remains open to us. If G has been successfully vindicated, then we must grant that a person who says 'I see. . .' tell us in part that he seems to see some object. But, now, in at least most instances in which a person believes firmly that he does see the object which he seems to see, it would be pointless for him to withhold the additional information (whatever it may be) which is conveyed by 'I see. . .'. A person who believes that he sees a certain object, and says only that he seems to see it, deliberately withholds information from us – tells us part, but only part, of what he believes to be the case. And ordinarily there is simply no reason for anyone to do this. Of course, one may not be motivated to say anything at all; we do not often find it worthwhile to report that we see the objects which in fact we see. But, when a person is motivated to report that he sees a certain object, he is generally motivated to tell us what he believes to be the whole story (that he sees the object) and not just a part of it (that he seems to see the object). It is for this reason that a person who says 'I seem to see. . .' is ordinarily understood not to be fully convinced that he sees the object which he mentions.

   An analogy may be useful at this point. If I wish to report that I went for a brisk walk this afternoon, I shall not, at least ordinarily, say, 'I moved my legs this afternoon'. To say the latter is to tell only part of the story, while to say 'I went for a brisk walk' is to tell the part told by 'I moved my legs' and more. And ordinarily there would be no reason for me to wish to tell only the part of the story about my moving my legs, even though I know that the whole story is true. It is for this reason that, were I to say, 'I moved my legs this afternoon', I should generally be understood to be indicating that my ability to walk had been in some way impaired – just as a person who says 'I seem to see . . .' is generally understood to doubt or disbelieve that he really sees the object to which he refers.

It goes without saying that, if the foregoing explanation is correct, then it is not self-contradictory or in any way absurd to say that we seem to see objects whenever we see them. Indeed, my explanation embodies a repudiation of the thesis that it is self-contradictory or absurd to say this, since it involves the claim that seeming to see is a logically necessary condition of seeing. Philosophers who are convinced that 'I see . . .' says something which is in some sense logically incompatible with what is said by 'I seem to see . . .' will of course reject the explanation which I have offered (along with G). But they cannot argue for their position on the ground that any of the analyses of 'I seem to see . . .' which I have been considering are correct (and if there are other, at least speciously plausible, analyses, we need to be told what they are); nor can they argue for their position by saying that, unless some such analysis were adequate, it would be impossible to present a credible account of the fact that 'I seem to see X' is not generally uttered except when the speaker doubts or disbelieves that he really sees X.

7.8 I have formulated argument G in terms of the (ordinary) language of seeming, but it can be formulated as well in terms of the (ordinary) language of appearing. In particular, 'It appears as if such and such is the case' does not mean 'Maybe such and such is the case', since there are situations in which one can say with perfect propriety, for example, 'I know that it appears to you as though he is recovering from his illness, but, unfortunately this is mere appearance; he is still very ill'. Nor can we construe 'It appears as if such and such is the case' as typically stating that the speaker is inclined to believe that such and such is the case, since there are circumstances in which one can say with linguistic correctness, for example, 'It appears to me as though I am seeing a rabbit on the chair, but I am inclined to believe that (what) I am really seeing (is) a cat there'. The 'but' in this locution is used to *contrast* the second conjunct with the first, and, hence, it would be wrong to interpret that locution as an expression of ambivalence. Finally, 'It appears to me as if I am seeing. . .' clearly does not mean the same as 'I doubt and/or disbelieve that I am seeing. . .' since, though I can doubt and/or disbelieve that I (really) see a rabbit on the chair when in fact I (really) see a cat there, there are surely cases in which it is *false* that it *appears* to me as if I am seeing a rabbit on the chair when in fact I see a cat there. (Indeed, that is *normally* false.)

It is, of course, the case that a person does not normally say 'It appears to me as if I am seeing X' unless she doubts or disbelieves that she is seeing X. However, since we can plainly substitute 'appears' for 'seems' in argument G, there is an explanation of this fact, which does not entail that this sentence is used *just* to express doubt or disbelief: argument G establishes in effect that its appearing to a person as if she sees X is a logically necessary condition of her seeing X. So if she firmly believes that she (really) sees X and utters the contemplated locution, she does something analogous to what I would be doing were I to say to you 'I moved my legs rapidly between 3:00 p.m. and 4:00 p.m. this afternoon', when in fact I know that I had effortlessly taken a brisk walk then. Since my taking a brisk walk logically entails my rapidly moving my legs, there would be no reason for me to tell only *that* part of the story, if my walking had not been in some way impaired, or I had not been lying on my back and moving my legs in the air (or so on). Still, what I said would have been, strictly speaking, true. And if argument G is sound, it is strictly speaking true, when I veridically see X, that it appears to me as if I am seeing X, though there would be no reason for me to tell just the latter part of the story unless I doubted or disbelieved that I (really) saw X.

7.9   D. M. Armstrong agrees there is such a thing as 'perception without belief or inclination to believe'.[5] Though he talks about 'perceptions' rather than 'seeming perceptions' what he says is clearly applicable to the latter; and, for convenience, I shall translate Armstrong's 'perceptions' into the language of seeming perceptions.

Armstrong argues as follows: When we seem to perceive objects, even without an inclination to believe that we do,

> an event still occurs in our mind, an event which can be described as one that would be the acquiring of a belief but for the existence

of other, contrary beliefs that we already hold. The event might perhaps be called the acquiring of a *potential belief.* We come to be in a certain state which would be a belief state but for the inhibiting effect of other, contrary beliefs. In this way [seeming] perceptions without belief or inclination to believe might be fitted into our analysis.[6]

Now, this cannot accommodate skeptics such as Sextus Empiricus, who, though they seem to perceive objects, hold no beliefs and *a fortiori* no inhibiting beliefs (not even the belief that their seeming perceptions are nonveridical). But Armstrong anticipates this kind of objection. He imagines a critic who argues as follows:

It is at best a contingent fact of psychology that '[seeming] belief' is an event that would be the acquiring of a belief but for the possession of other, independent, beliefs. We can quite well imagine the occurrence of [seeming] perceptions that involve no acquiring of belief at all, even though contrary beliefs about the world are absent.[7]

And he adds that 'in answer to this I say that, if [seeming] perceptions did occur which were not even the acquiring of potential beliefs . . . they would be events *like* the acquiring of beliefs or potential beliefs about the world'.[8]

Now, this part of Armstrong's analysis needs considerable elaboration-*cum*-defense. If Armstrong were justified in simply maintaining that seeming perceptions which are neither the acquiring of beliefs nor the acquiring of potential beliefs are nonetheless like seeming perceptions which essentially involve belief acquisition, then successful explications of philosophically interesting concepts would be impossible. Suppose that I embark on an explication of the concept of knowledge, that you provide a counter-example, and that I try to accommodate it by claiming that instances of knowledge of the kind mentioned in your counter-example can be analyzed as being like, but not exactly like, normal instances. If I were then to refuse to tell you the precise respect in which the alleged likeness obtains, this would clearly be a flagrant violation of acceptable philosophical procedure.

However, Armstrong apparently anticipates this objection as well. He attempts to clarify the alleged respect in which perceptions without belief or potential belief are like seeming perception-*cum*-belief or potential belief:

> The nature of [seeming] perceptions without even the acquiring of potential belief should now be clear. . . The event involved is of the belief-acquiring sort, but, like poison [which is] insufficiently concentrated to poison, not even potential belief is acquired.[9]

The poison to which Armstrong refers is diluted by a harmless liquid and, hence, rendered ineffective. But his analogy is not strong enough. Either the diluted poison resembles nondiluted poison with respect to its molecular structure, or 'poison' does not accurately describe it, and, hence, all we know about it is that it was once poison. But it is surely not open to Armstrong to maintain that beliefless-seeming perceptions all involve something which was once belief acquisition or potential belief acquisition but is no more. Moreover, the claim that beliefless-seeming perceptions are like the allegedly standard ones in that they involve belief is patently inconsistent. And, again, if Armstrong were to maintain here that beliefless-seeming perceptions essentially involve something which is 'significantly similar' to belief (as diluted poison is significantly similar to undiluted poison with respect to its molecular structure), then we would be justified in rejecting his claim until he told us precisely what that something is. (I use 'significantly similar' because there is, of course, some respect in which anything is similar to everything. Thus, for example, everything resembles everything else with respect to self-identity. However, philosophical explication would break down if counter-examples could be accommodated in terms of just any kind of resemblance, no matter how weak.)

7.10 So much for argument G. Let us turn now to the question of whether our beliefs about our physical environment are rooted in certain mental states of ours, namely, our seeming perceptions. The following is an argument that they are.

Presumably, everyone would agree that, normally, when I come to believe that I am veridically seeing an object O, at moment M, something is the *cause* of my holding that belief. Now, in normal circumstances, the only candidates for that cause are my veridical seeing of O at M or my seeming to see O at M or both. Some philosophers have held that the object which I am veridically seeing causes my seeming to see it, which in turn causes my belief that I am veridically seeing that object at M. But let us, for simplicity, discuss just the question of whether it is my veridical seeing of O at M or my seeming to see O at M which *directly* causes my belief that I veridically see O at M. (O itself is plainly not a *direct* cause of that belief.)

Now I have shown that whenever I veridically see an object, O, at place P at moment M, I also seem to see *something* at place P at moment M. And suppose that it is not O which I seem to see. Then, if I am rational, my belief that I am veridically seeing *precisely* O at moment M is caused (a) by my seeming to see some object *other* than O (call it 'O'') at M and (b) by my belief that *seeming* to see O', in the abnormal circumstances in which I find myself, is a reliable indicator of the fact that I am *veridically* seeing (*really* seeing), not O', but O. For I would be irrational, were my belief that I am veridically seeing O at P at M based *simply* on my seeming to see O' at P at M. And it is surely reasonable to conclude that when, in *normal* circumstances, a person believes that she veridically sees O and seems to see (not O' but) O, the direct cause of that belief is her seeming to see O.

It will not do to object here that it may be a person's *belief* that she seems to see O which causes her to believe that she veridically sees O, but not her seeming to see O *per se*. For just as her (rational) belief that she is veridically seeing O is in need of some cause or other, so, too, her (rational) belief that she *seems* to see O is in need of some cause or other; and surely the best candidate is her seeming to see O *per se*.

It follows that a person's rational belief that she veridically sees O is, normally, causally grounded in her seeming to see O, and that, when it is not, it is *partly* caused by her seeming to see some object other than O. There is yet another reason for holding that it is false that, if I am rational and believe that I veridically see O at M, then that belief is directly caused by my veridical seeing of O at M. For I could be perfectly rational and believe that I am veridically seeing O at M, even though I was only *seeming* to see O at M. This would be the case if, say, I were tricked by a psychologist of perception. But the only candidate in this case for a direct cause of my belief that I veridically see O at M is my (merely) *seeming* to see O at M.

And it is surely incredible that, though in cases, in which I rationally, but falsely, believe that I veridically see O at M, my belief is directly caused by my seeming to see O, while in cases, in which I rationally, and *truly* believe, that I veridically see O at M, my belief is *not* directly caused by my seeming to see O at M, but rather by my veridical seeing of O at M. The envisaged proposition is analogous to the claim that, when I am caused to believe rationally, but falsely, that Smith murdered Jones, my seeing Smith leave Jones's house shortly after the murder causes that belief, but that when I believe rationally, but *truly*, that Smith murdered Jones, in a case in which I was not an eyewitness to the murder, but saw Smith leaving Jones's house shortly after the murder, the latter is not a cause of my belief that Smith murdered Jones, though Smith's actually having murdered Jones *simpliciter* is such a cause.

It follows that unless a person's belief that she veridically sees O is epistemically grounded in her seeming to see O, then she is not warranted in believing that she sees O. For (with a proviso to be added shortly) if a person is caused to believe that a certain proposition, p, is true solely by a certain cause C, then either C is also a good *reason* for her to believe that p is true, or she is not *justified* in believing that p is true. Thus, if my seeing Smith leaving the house shortly after the murder was committed is the sole cause of my believing that Smith committed the murder, then either it is also a good reason for me to hold that belief or I am not justified in holding that belief. No doubt, I would be justified, in the circumstances, in believing that Smith committed the murder if I had some other good reason for holding that belief. But *ex hypothesi* my seeing Smith leaving the house shortly after the murder is the only cause of my believing that Smith committed the murder, and *a fortiori* this other 'good reason' is not also a cause. But R can be a good reason for me to believe that p is true only if it is a *cause* of my so believing.

Here it may be said that my seeing Smith leaving the house shortly after the murder simply is not the only cause of my belief that he committed the murder – that, for example, the brain processes which are causally connected with that perception are *also* a cause. But the answer is simply that it is the only cause with respect to which I do not also require evidence. Or, at any rate, that *would* be the answer if my belief that I saw Smith leaving the house were not epistemically grounded in my belief that I *seemed* to see Smith leaving the house. And I submit that the envisaged analogy gives us reason to believe that it *is* so grounded.

We need to qualify the claim that if E is the sole unevidenced cause of my belief that a given proposition, p, is true, and E is not an epistemic ground of my belief, then I am not justified in believing that p is true. For my belief in a *properly basic* proposition, such as 7 + 5 = 12 might have as its sole unevidenced cause my having been told so by a raving lunatic or, more precisely, by my *seeming* to see and hear him; and yet, even though this cause *per se* is not also an adequate epistemic ground of my belief that 7 + 5 = 12, I would nonetheless be justified in holding that belief. But we need simply to qualify the principle by saying that it holds true for all beliefs *except beliefs in properly basic propositions*. And since it is obviously true that sometimes, when I seem to see an object, O, and, as a consequence, *believe* that I really see O, my belief turns out to be false, and, hence, *not* properly basic, it is also obviously true that *no* belief that I am really seeing O is properly basic for me.

Here it may be said that this argument is like the argument that, say, the proposition that 4 x 60 = 240 is not properly basic, since we sometimes make arithmetical mistakes. But I submit that if we made arithmetical mistakes as *often* as we make perceptual mistakes (that is, in dreams), then we would have to agree that no arithmetical propositions are properly basic.

7.11  Consider the following epistemic principle: when we infer the existence of a given thing, T, from a given datum, D, then either (a) we have been noninferentially acquainted with T-like things in the past and also non-inferentially acquainted with their being conjoined with D-like things or (b) in cases in which condition (a) is not satisfied either there is a scientific justification of the inference (as in the case of, say, inferences to quarks) or there is some other respectable argument which validates the inference.

Call this principle 'P'. I submit that P is sufficiently broad in scope so that anyone, who makes the common sense distinction (so often drawn in courts of law) between beliefs based on direct acquaintance (on 'personal experience' ) and beliefs based on inference, will accept it.

Now let us look at causal realism, the thesis that when we infer that we are veridically seeing a desk on the basis of our seeming to see, say, a desk, what we infer is that there is a mind-independent physical object, O, which is the cause of the mental state (call it 'M' ) which is described by 'I seem to see a desk'. (The reason for the qualifer, 'mind-independent,' will become clear in Appendix I.) In view of principle P, either we have been, or are, noninferentially acquainted with O, or with things of the same kind, or there is some justification of our inference from M to O, or the inference is unwarranted. But the following, familiar argument casts doubt on the claim that we are, or ever have been, noninferentially acquainted with O or with things of the same kind. Being in mental states, which are very similar to M, is not *always* a case of being noninferentially acquainted with objects which are very similar to O. For mental states like M are frequently the constituents of dreams and hallucinations. Nor is there always a phenomenological difference between M-like mental states which are, and M-like mental states which are not, the constituents of dreams and hallucinations. For rational people can mistake the one kind of mental state for the other. It may be said here that rational people never mistake M-like states which are not constituents of dreams and hallucinations for M-like states which are, and that this shows that when people mistake the latter states for the former ones, they are irrationally overlooking a phenomenological difference. But surely a clever psychologist could make a perfectly rational person believe that she was merely seeming to see, say, an apple by telling her (a) that he has given her a hallucinogenic drug and (b) that there is no apple in the vicinity. And it is equally easy to imagine a rational person's being tricked into believing that an experience which was still fresh in her mind was in fact a dream experience. But if there is no significant phenomenological difference between M and M-like mental states which are constituents of dream and hallucinations then, since the latter are plainly not instances of noninferential acquaintance with O-like objects, we have a plausible inductive argument for the conclusion that M itself is not an instance of non-inferential acquaintance with O. (And if someone rejects this argument, she still needs to tell us how we can know, on any given occasion, that a given mental state is an instance of direct acquaintance with a physical object rather than a constituent of a dream or hallucination.)

It follows that, in view of P, the causal realist needs a sound argument, scientific or otherwise, which will warrant the inference from M to O. But it looks as if there is no scientific theory, which warrants the inference from M to the existence of a mind-independent, physical cause of M. Scientific theories do, of course, back many inferences, to things with which we are not directly acquainted, for example, inferences to quarks from the data produced by particle accelerators. But I submit that there is no analogous, sound scientific theory which gets us just from M to a mind-independent cause of M.

Here the following argument may be advanced: 'Scientific theories predict, among other things, that if an observable physical event, $E_1$, occurs, then another observable physical event, $E_2$, will occur. So they predict, in effect, that if I see $E_1$ occurring, then I will see $E_2$ occurring. But since, as Dore has argued, it is normally true that when I see $E_1$, I am in the mental state picked out by 'I seem to see $E_1$' and when I see $E_2$, I am in the mental state picked out by 'I seem to see $E_2$', scientific theories predict that things with which I am directly acquainted, namely, the envisaged mental states, will be conjoined. And since I can check up on that prediction, I can *verify* or falsify those theories just by reference to those mental states. Hence, scientific theories do, after all, justify inferences from seeming to see to a mind-independent physical world; and so there is no special problem about how they can warrant inferences from M to a mind-independent, physical cause of M.

There are a number of things wrong with this argument. First, it cannot, as it stands, account for the fact that even though a physical event, $E_1$, is constantly conjoined with another physical event, $E_2$, my seeming-to-see $E_1$ may well not be constantly conjoined with my seeming-to-see $E_2$. This happens frequently in dreams. And, second, the argument is successful *only if* the various observations on which the envisaged theories (the putative predictors of our seemings-to-see) are based are all such that the claim to be making them could be similarly justified by *other* scientific theories. But that starts us on an unacceptable regress: we are not in possession of an *indefinitely large number* of observation-backing (and backed) scientific theories.

Some scientific theories of perception in effect predict that if certain observations are made, then certain seemings-to-see (commonly called 'sensations' ) will occur, without requiring that those sensations be ingredients of observations. But like scientific theories which are not theories of perception, they do not successfully warrant an inference from the sensations which are constituents of the observations on which they rely just to the conclusion that those observations are in fact being made.

But why should we not look at the matter this way: We know that some scientific theories successfully predict those mental states which are picked out by 'I seem to see . . .', and, hence, we have evidence for *them*, and so we *can argue inductively* that *most* scientific theories are sound? But even if we set aside the problem which we have seen that dreaming presents for the claim that some scientific theories accurately predict our seemings-to-see, there is *another* problem, namely, the problem as to what is to count as a sound scientific theory. One indispensable criterion is that it be backed by considerable observational evidence (unlike, say, astrology), and in view of that consideration, the putative inductive argument is question-begging, since it *presupposes* that we know, with respect to many theories, that then are adequately backed by observations.

Another reply is that the envisaged argument succeeds only if scientific theories which accurately predict our seemings-to-see are *scientifically basic*, in the sense that, though they are not in need of support by other kinds of scientific theory, these latter theories are in need of support by them. And I submit that those scientific theories which do accurately predict our seemings-to-see, are not more apt to be independent of verification by other *kinds* of scientific theory, then are the latter to be epistemically independent of the former.

7.12   But doesn't science assert that my seeming to see my desk normally has a mind-independent, physical desk as one of its causes? And isn't it irrational to reject science?

The answer is that it is not irrational to reject scientific realism and, hence, it is not irrational to reject scientific *causal* realism – as opposed to a pragmatic or instrumentalist interpretation of science. I submit that scientific causal realism is based on the assumption that we do not, and need not, base an inference to the existence of, say, a mind-independent desk in my study on mental states which are picked out by 'I seem to see. . .', and *a fortiori* we do not need a scientific justification of that inference. In short, I submit that the scientific causal realist assumes that we are directly (that is, non-inferentially) acquainted with my desk when in fact we see it. All that we *need* to infer are those *parts* of the desk with which we are *not* directly acquainted, that is, electrons, quarks and the like. And it would, of course, be folly to maintain that there are no highly justified scientific theories which back *those* inferences. But, as I have been arguing, this model is mistaken. We are not noninferentially acquainted with my desk and objects like my desk. And there is no scientific theory which backs the inference *just* from my seeming to see my desk to my desk, as there is a scientific theory which backs the inference to the microstructure of my desk once we have somehow gotten to a mind-independent desk.

Indeed, scientific causal realism, with respect to my desk, is incoherent, since it starts out by positing direct perception of a brown, solid object and ends up by affirming that the object is colorless and consists mainly of empty space – and, even worse, that when I see my desk at any given moment, M, I am directly acquainted with something which existed slightly before M. (In the case of my seeing stars at M, I am directly acquainted with something which existed millions or billions of years before M.)

In this connection, it will be instructive to look at the so-called 'principle of credulity', promulgated by C.D. Broad and, more recently, by Richard Swinburne, which asserts that, when I seem to see a given kind of thing, O, I am warranted in believing that I do, indeed, see O, unless there is some reason to think otherwise. It might appear at first glance that this principle provides the scientific causal realist with an alternative to the claim that scientific theories alone will justify inferences to mind-independent causes of our seeming to see.

But this is mere appearance. Suppose that, having the principle of credulity in mind, I say 'This tomato *looks* red, and I have no good reason for thinking that it isn't red. Therefore, I am justified in believing that it *is* red.' Then if by 'is red' I imply that its redness is unrelated to the way it would look to alert and enquiring, sighted people in sunlight, then scientific realism tells us that this is false. So the principle of credulity either obliges us to conclude that we *do* have reason to believe that the tomato, despite appearances, isn't red or to adopt a dispositional theory of what it is for a physical object to be red.

However, such Lockean dispositional analyses are sufficiently popular, so that many philosophers will not want to reject scientific realism-*cum*-the principle of credulity for the reason just presented.

But similar considerations hold true for 'is not mainly composed of empty space'. And it is surely implausible that, when I attribute *that* property to my desk, I am attributing to it a disposition to appear *not* to be composed mainly of empty space, even though science tells us that my desk is, in reality, so constituted.[10] This is no more plausible than the claim that attributing being the same person as Hitler to someone is claiming that he *looks* like Hitler, whether in fact he *is* Hitler.

Scientific realism also negates the application of the principle of credulity to my claim that it looks to me as though I am seeing a star *which currently exists*, when, in fact, given scientific realism it went super-nova billions of years before now. The scientific realist may want to say here that it does not look to me as if I am seeing a heavenly body which *currently exists*, but rather that it looks to me as if I am seeing *light waves* which do, in fact, currently exist. But then, since he denies that, when it looks to me as if I am seeing, say, my desk occupying my study at moment M, what I am seeing exists *precisely at M*, he needs to tell us why seeing stars is seeing light waves, but seeing desks is not. (Needless to say, if all that we ever see are light waves, then the principle of credulity is of no epistemic value.)

In short, given scientific realism, we *may* have reason to believe that, say, ripe tomatoes are not red, despite the fact that they appear to be red, and we *surely* have reason to believe that ripe tomatoes are mainly composed of empty space, despite the fact that they appear not to be. But then what beliefs about the ripe tomato *are* warranted by its appearance in conjunction with the principle of credulity? The answer, for the scientific realist, has to be 'We have to rely entirely on science to find out whether, when an object appears to have a given property, $P$, we nonetheless have reason to believe that it does not have P'. But that entails that we have to rely entirely on scientific realism to find out on any given occasion, whether the principle of credulity applies on that occasion. And that entails in turn that the claim that the principle of credulity supports scientific realism is flagrantly circular.

One might, of course formulate the principle of credulity as follows: 'Whenever I seem to see an object, there is a *prima facie* case on behalf of my seeing something, O, which resembles what I seem to see *to the extent that science tells us that it does*.' But obviously the principle of credulity, thus formulated, does not give the scientific realist a datum with which to start. For he has to rely on science in order to discover the true *nature* of that datum.

My argument, in brief, is this. The scientific causal realist claims in effect that all of our seemings-to-see of physical objects and events are (at best) *partially hallucinatory*, and, hence, so, too are all of our putative seeings of physical objects and events, but that the correct theory of the true nature of what we perceive can be based on these (at best) partial hallucinations. Perhaps this would be acceptable, if I could determine the extent to which I am partially hallucinating when I seem to see my desk. But it would be obviously circular to maintain both that scientific realism can tell me that *and* that scientific realism is epistemically *based* on partial hallucinations.

Finally, the causal realist may want to argue here as follows: 'Set *scientific* theories aside. The hypothesis that there is a mind-independent *nonscientific* desk in my study which will cause me to see my desk, upon seeing my study, successfully predicts that when I see my study, I will see my desk, and hence, that if I *seem* to see my study, then I will *seem* to see my desk. And, hence, those seemings-to-see give me evidence for the envisaged hypothesis.' But surely if we *reject* the claim that *science* tells us about the mind-independent causation of our seemings-to-see – if we reject *scientific* causal realism – then accepting *non*scientific causal realism is, in effect, rejecting science. I shall have more to say about this in 7.10.

Berkeley maintained in effect that we are never warranted in inferring the existence of a physical thing, T, from a given datum, D, unless we have at some time been noninferentially acquainted with T. He did not qualify this claim by adding 'unless the inference is backed by a scientific theory', and it has appeared to some as through this is an instance of eighteenth century scientific naiveté. But if I am right about scientific causal realism, Berkeley did not *need* to qualify in that way, since we *cannot* in fact make warranted inferences, which are backed by scientific theories, to parts of the physical world, with which we have never been noninferentially acquainted. It follows that there must be some nonscientific way of justifying claims to have made those observations which science successfully predicts. A prescientific, phenomenalist justification of our observation claims has been the classical, epistemological alternative to causal realism. In Chapter 8 I shall discuss that theory at length. But first I shall end the present chapter by (1) setting out yet another reason for doubting scientific realism and, hence, scientific *causal* realism, and (2) examining a recent defense of Wittgenstein's famous dictum that there can be no such thing as a 'private language', from which it has been thought to follow that the egocentric predicament of the classical epistemologists is unreal.

7.13 The advocate of scientific realism frequently argues as follows: 'The predictive fruitfulness of so-called scientific theoretical constructs is a proof of their mind-independent reality. The concept of, say, a quark wouldn't be predictively fruitful unless there really were mind-independent quarks – just as the concept of a mind-independent, colorless desk, which consists almost entirely of empty space, wouldn't be predictively fruitful unless there really were such a thing. But it is surely doubtful that Berkeley was being wrongheaded when he denied the claim that, since Newton's infinitesimals are predictively fruitful, calculating devices, they really exist. Moreover, as is well known, predictive fruitfulness alone is not an adequate validation of scientific theory. We need simplicity as well. The geocentric theory made pretty much the same predictions as the heliocentric theory does. But it was inferior because more complex, that is, it involved epicycles. It will not do to say here that it was inferior, not because it was more complex, but because it falsely predicted epicycles. For, if we set complexity aside, then how do we know that that was a *false* prediction?

But now why should the simplicity of a theory be a proof of its truth? It is sometimes said that we are warranted in holding that the universe really is simple. But, first, what is the proof of this? It would be obviously circular for the scientific realist to maintain that the fact that those theories which we adopt are relatively simple shows, in conjunction with the fact that they are true, that the universe is simple. And, anyway, just how simple should we take the universe to be? Once we start positing simple universes, why should we suppose that the simplicity of the real universe exactly matches the simplicity of scientific theories? Again, it would be circular for the scientific realist to maintain that, since we know that our theories are true, we know that the universe is *just* as simple as they are.

It follows from these considerations that it must be false that the best explanation of the predictive fruitfulness of a scientific theory is that the theoretical constructs, in terms of which it is formulated, have mind-independent reality. For relatively complex scientific theories may have the same *predictive* potential as relatively simple, but incompatible, scientific theories. (The geocentric and helio-centric theories are the classical example of this.)

I do not mean to claim here that there is *no* sense in which, say, heavy molecules are real. We can, after all, see them with the aid of an electron microscope. I am only trying to show that the scientific realist's claim that they have an entirely mind-independent existence is not viable. I shall return to this topic in the Appendix I.

7.14 Saul Kripke has recently set out an interpretation and tentative defense of Wittgenstein's famous thesis that there can be no private language, that is, that any individual who speaks an intelligible language must be part of a *community* of language users, each of whose speech habits are an indispensable criterion for the correctness of any other individual's speech habits. Kripke's argument goes roughly as follows: 'The only way in which an individual can determine that an object is not 'grue,' where 'grue' = 'past objects were grue iff they were (then) green, while present objects are grue iff they are (now) blue' [11] is to observe that his fellow rule-following language-users did *not* in the past call objects which are now blue 'green'. There is no such thing as a single individual's mental act of deciding once and for all to say that any objects which were green in the past and are now blue have changed color. For if a person held an image of green in his mind's eye and said 'I shall let that image determine the way I shall go on using 'green' in the future' he would, barring public usage, have no way of determining that the image was not in reality an image of grue.'

Let us, for convenience, call Kripke 'Kripkenstein'. His argument applies to discourse about visual seeming perceptions of green and blue, only if (a) their *esse* is *percipi* and (b) one individual's visual seeming perceptions of those colors cannot be numerically identical with another individual's visual seeming perceptions, so that one individual cannot check up on whether any other individual is using 'green' or 'blue' correctly when she says 'I am seeming to see a green (or blue) object' by simply having that very same visual seeming perception. But in fact (a) and (b) are clearly true. For it is surely incredible that visual seeming perceptions are (as they plainly are) mind-dependent and private, *qua* ingredients of dreams and hallucinations, but mind-independent, public objects, *qua* ingredients in veridical perceptions.

However, Kripkenstein's argument is demonstrably flawed. For either Kripkenstein is taking 'green' and 'blue' as primitive, and defining 'grue' in terms of these primitives, or he is in effect admitting that we have no idea what 'grue' means, and, hence, admitting in effect that we do not know what problem he is trying to solve. Suppose, then, that he is doing the former. Then, given his basic thesis – that I cannot speak a private language – he is committed to the view that, if there were an egocentric predicament, his putative refutation of it would not be intelligible.

Here it may be said that, since that refutation obviously *is* intelligible, I can know that in fact there *is* no egocentric predicament. But it is surely *generally* true that if the efficacy of a putative refutation of a given thesis, T, has, as a presupposition, as well as a consequence, that T is false, then that alleged refutation should be rejected. And it is far from clear why Kripkenstein's putative refutation of the thesis that there is an egocentric predicament should be thought to be an exception.

But how *could* a child be able to speak a language if he were not taught by members of a language-using community? The answer is that *as a matter of empirical fact* he could not, but that it is *logically possible* that he could. For since Kripkenstein's critique of the doctrine of private seeming perceptions is a failure, it cannot cogently support the thesis that 'All of my seeming perceptions are *mere* seeming perceptions (all appearances are illusory)' is unintelligible.

A simpler argument that it is, in fact, unintelligible is that, say, 'I seem to see a red tomato' means something like 'I seem to see what people normally see when they really see a red tomato.' But that argument is cogent only if it is logically impossible for me to have the concept of a person's really seeing a red tomato, unless some person or persons have in fact really seen a red tomato. And I submit that that claim is plausible only if we equate empirical impossibility with logical impossibility.

# 8

# Theistic Phenomenalism: An Alternative Causal Theory of Perception

8.1   When I seem to see my study and I also seem to see my desk in it, I am normally justified in inferring that all or most alert and enquiring beings who were in the mental state described by 'I seem to see...', where the dots are filled in by an exact description of the physical environment of my desk, would seem to see my desk. The question arises, then, as to whether, when I conclude that I am really seeing my desk in my study, this latter conclusion is, or should be taken to be, equivalent to the former conclusion. An affirmative answer to this question is made tempting by the argument of Chapter 6 that I cannot justifiably conclude that a mind-independent desk is the cause of my seeming to see my desk.

We need, then, to look at some objections to the envisaged version of phenomenalism.

8.2   It may be said that, since my desk may be destroyed or removed from my study shortly after my seeming to see it, at a given moment M, the phenomenalist is *not* justified in inferring that all or most alert and enquiring beings would seem to see it *after M*, even given that the environment condition were satisfied.

But the phenomenalist can reply that she is entitled to make that inference if in fact my desk has not been destroyed or removed from my study after M. And she can maintain that my desk's not having been destroyed or removed from my study after M consists of its being false that alert and enquiring beings, who were in the mental state described by 'I seem to see...' where the dots are filled in by an exact description of the environment of my desk, would *not* seem to see my desk being destroyed or removed from my study *after M*.

8.3   It may be said that, while it's being the case that all or most alert and enquiring beings would seem to see my desk, given that the environment condition were satisfied, may be *sufficient* for there being a desk in my study, it is not clearly necessary; since it is not clearly the case that my desk would not be in my study if, say, only half of alert and enquiring beings would seem to see it, if the environment condition were satisfied.

But the phenomenalist has a reply. She can maintain that she is giving us a *theory*, not a *definition*, of what it is for my desk to be in my study, and, that *qua* theoretician, she is justified in stipulating that it is necessary, as well as sufficient, that all or most alert and enquiring beings would seem to see my desk, if the environment condition were satisfied, by considerations of theoretical simplicity. I shall return to this topic in the next section.

8.4   The phenomenalist must account for the case in which I conclude that, in the circumstances in which I find myself, my seeming perception of O', for example, a bent oar in water, is a reliable indicator of the fact that what I am seeing is, in reality, O, for example, a straight oar. She must tell us what seeing (really seeing) a straight oar consists of in *this* case. And it is clear that she cannot claim that it consists of its being true that all or most alert and enquiring sighted beings, who are in the mental state reported by 'I seem to see...', where the dots are filled in by an exact description of the environment of the oar, would seem to see a straight oar. The reason, put in nonphenomenalist language, is simply that alert and enquiring sighted beings, *who found themselves in my present environment*, would seem to see a *bent* oar.

But the phenomenalist can reply roughly as follows: In the envisaged circumstances, I have, on the basis of past experience, reason to reject the inference to the envisaged phenomenalist conditional. However, I have no reason to reject an inference just to this less qualified phenomenalist conditional: 'All or most alert and enquiring beings, who were in the mental state described by 'I seem to see...,' where the dots are filled in by an exact description of the environment of the oar, would seem to see *an oar simpliciter*.' And, to capture the situation in greater detail, I can infer further that they would seem to see an oar which merely looks bent to them, in the sense that they would not seem to see a bent oar, but rather a straight one, were they in the mental state described by 'I seem to see. . .', where the dots are filled in by an exact description of the environment of the oar, which is exactly similar to its present environment, except for the oar's being submerged in water.

It should be added that if in fact I am not suffering an optical illusion, but, for some idiosyncratic reason, when I seem to see, say, a rat, what I am really seeing is an old shoe, then, given that I know that this is the case, I *would* be justified in inferring that most *other* alert and enquiring beings, who were in the mental state described by 'I seem to see. . .', where the dots are filled in by an exact description of the environment of the old shoe, would seem to see (not a rat but) an old shoe.

I would not, in the envisaged circumstances, be warranted in inferring that *all* other alert and enquiring beings would seem to see an old shoe, if the environment condition were satisfied. I would not be justified in inferring that there would not be even one, or a few, alert and enquiring beings who, for idiosyncratic reasons similar to those which pertain to me, would seem to see something *other* than an old shoe if the environment condition were satisfied.

So the phenomenalist cannot stipulate that it is a necessary condition of my (really) seeing an old shoe that *all* alert and enquiring beings would seem to see an old shoe, given that the environment condition were satisfied. (Indeed, in the contemplated case, I violate that condition.) But I think that the phenomenalist *would* be justified in stipulating that it's being the case that *most* alert and enquiring beings would seem to see an old shoe, if the environment condition were satisfied, is a necessary condition for our all (really) seeing an old shoe. For it is false that *most* alert and enquiring beings would seem to see an old shoe *for idiosyncratic* reasons, and, hence, one cannot argue on *that* ground that the '*most* alert and enquiring beings' condition cannot be *sufficient*.

8.5 I have just argued in effect against the objection that the phenomenalist cannot accommodate optical illusions and partial hallucinations. But more needs to be said about the Chisholm-like objection that she cannot accommodate partial hallucinations without falling back on the concept of a 'normal' perceiver, which cannot be phenomenalistically construed.

Consider the following, Chisholm-like argument: 'Suppose that before a given time, t, there was a rare brain tumor which caused those few alert and enquiring people who suffered from it to be incapable of seeming to see desks, and *a fortiori* to be incapable of seeming to see my desk upon seeming to see the rest of my study, even though most alert and enquiring beings *would* seem to see my desk upon seeming to see the rest of my study. Then it would be irrational not to conclude that the former people were, or would be, negatively hallucinated with respect to Dore's desk.

'But now suppose further that, at some time after t, almost all alert and enquiring beings contracted this tumor. Then surely they, too, would be negatively hallucinated with respect to Dore's desk, even though, given Dore's version of phenomenalism, a necessary condition of the existence of my desk in my study would not be satisfied.

'So the phenomenalist needs to formulate her conditional in terms of 'normal' alert and enquiring beings. But then 'S is a normal, alert and enquiring being' must be construed as making a claim about S's neurophysiological state. And if the phenomenalist tries to construe this claim phenomenalistically, then, since she must fall back on *normal* alert and enquiring beings once again, she is started on a vicious regress.

'The phenomenalist may, of course, maintain here that people who suffer from the envisaged brain tumor are *a fortiori not* alert and enquiring beings. But then she will have the same problem about construing 'alert and enquiring' phenomenalistically that she has about construing 'normal' phenomenalistically.'

My answer to this objection can be put very succinctly: The criterion of a person's normalcy is, not her physiological or neurophysiological condition, but rather her *being in a considerable majority of alert and enquiring beings with respect to what she does, or would, seem to see.* Let me spell this out. Consider the claim that a brain tumor might cause most alert and enquiring beings to be incapable of seeming to see my desk upon seeming to see the rest of my study. Unless this claim is true, then the envisaged objection collapses. But in fact the claim entails that there *is* a desk in my study, even though most alert and enquiring beings would fail to seem to see it, even when they seemed to see the rest of my study. For if there *is* no desk in my study, then neither a brain tumor, nor any *other* physiological state, can *cause* people to fail to *see* it there, and *a fortiori* neither a brain tumor, nor any other physiological state can be a cause of people's failing to *seem to* see it there. So the contemplated claim is question-begging; and, hence, so is the envisaged objection.

The claim that if there is no desk in my study, then no physiological or neurophysiological condition of mine, can cause me to fail to *seem* to see it there is in need of qualification. Such a condition might counteract a drug which would *otherwise* cause me *merely* to seem to see it there. But this is a problem for the phenomenalist only if the drug might cause *most* alert and enquiring beings merely to seem to see my desk upon seeming to see my study. And that claim also begs the questions against my version of phenomenalism. For if my version of phenomenalism is correct, then most alert and enquiring beings being such that they would seem to see my desk, upon seeming to see the rest of my study is *sufficient* for the existence of the desk in my study. But *could* there be a drug which, if ingested, by most alert and enquiring beings, would cause them to be disposed to seem to see a desk upon seeming to see the rest of my study and, hence, given phenomenalism, would *cause* my desk to exist in my study? Isn't this claim strongly counter-intuitive? It will be convenient for me to put off answering this question until 8.13.

Let us look, once again, at the contemplated brain tumor. Here the following objection may be raised: 'Dore is committed to holding that the constant conjunction condition for causation is not satisfied here, that is, he is saying that, though the brain tumor is a cause of *some* alert and enquiring beings failing to seem to see my desk, it is *not* such a cause when it is contracted by a considerable majority.'

But in fact I am claiming that the tumor *is* constantly conjoined with a person's failing to seem to see my desk, *qua abnormality*; but not *qua normal state of affairs*. If there is resistance to this claim, I submit that it is because the expression 'brain tumor' *connotes* abnormality. But my point can be reexpressed as follows: What *would* be a brain tumor in the case of a minority of alert and enquiring beings, would *not* be a brain tumor, if it were a feature of the brains of all or most alert and enquiring beings. If we put my point *that* way, then there is no temptation to think that I am violating the constant conjunction condition.

8.6 There is more to be said about *merely* seeming to see. Suppose that there really is a desk in my study, so that it is true that most alert and enquiring beings would seem to see my desk upon being in the mental state described by 'I seem to see. . .', where the dots are filled in by an exact description of the rest of my study. And suppose that I am asleep and dreaming and that my dream consists in my vividly seeming to see my desk in my study. Then it follows from my phenomenalist theory of what it is for me really to see my desk in my study that I am, contrary to our perfectly feasible hypothesis, really seeing my desk in my study, instead of just dreaming that I am.

My phenomenalist theory is in need of modification, then. But a simple one is available: A necessary condition of my really seeing my desk in my study is that *my eyes be open and that* I be *within visual range of my desk*, where that consists of my body having a certain location, L, which is such that past experience has taught me that it is *not* the kind of location from which I cannot really see objects like my desk. My eyes being open and my body not having that location on a given occasion can then be analyzed phenomenalistically.

Or can it? The claim that S's eyes are open and his body has such and such a spatial location, L, is going to have to be taken by the phenomenalist to amount to its being the case that most other alert and enquiring beings, *who were within visual range of S's body*, would seem to see S's eyes being open and S's body occupying L. And isn't that unacceptably circular?

Let us, for simplicity, examine first the phenomenalist claim just that S's having a body consists roughly in its being the case that other alert and enquiring beings, *who were also embodied*, would seem to see S's body if they seemed to see such and such an environment. Is this a circular claim? I submit that it is not. For the phenomenalist can simply add that the embodiment of those other, alert and enquiring beings *consists in the same kind of thing*. Suppose that my being loved by a given non-neurotic person S, keeps me from being non-neurotic, and that S is also kept from being non-neurotic by being loved by a non-neurotic person, namely me. Surely this kind of symbiotic relationship sometimes obtains. And it is far from clear why the contemplated phenomenalist symbiotic relationship could not also obtain.

But, in order to give a phenomenalist construal of S's being within visual range of a given object, O, the phenomenalist simply needs to make 'other alert and enquiring beings would seem to see my body' read 'other alert and enquiring beings, who were within visual range of my body, would seem to see my body being within visual range of O; and their being within visual range of my body *consists in the same sort of thing'*.

There is another phenomenalist solution of the contemplated problem. Let us, for simplicity, suppose that there were just three alert and enquiring sentient beings, including me, and that two of them, A and B, seem to see my body being within visual range of O at a given moment M. The problem which leads to my visual range solution for my body, does not arise with respect to A's body and B's body. For it is false that both of their bodies might not be within visual range of my body at M, *because they were both asleep and dreaming*. If they were in fact asleep and dreaming, then their eyes would be closed and/or they would have a spatial location which is *not* within visual range of my body. But *that* amounts to it being the case that at least two of the three of us would seem to see B's body and A's body with their eyes closed and/or being in that different spatial location at M. But *ex hypothesi* A and B seem to see my body being within visual range of O, and, hence they do *not* seem to see *their* bodies occupying a location which is *not* within visual range of my body. Moreover, it is impossible for them to seem to see their eyes being closed at M when, at M, they seem to see something *other* than their eyes being closed.

Similar considerations apply to the case in which, though I am not asleep and dreaming, I am not within visual range of my desk and am suffering a hallucination in which I merely seem to see my desk.

For the sake of verbal economy, I shall henceforth omit the 'being within visual range' qualifier, that is, I shall leave it to the reader to fill it in mentally.

8.7 As is well known, statements like 'Dr Crippen murdered his wife in his study at time t' appear to resist their truth being phenomenalistically construed. The problem is that *if* alert and enquiring beings had been within visual range of Dr Crippen at time t, that is, if they had been potential witnesses to the murder, then Dr Crippen probably would *not* have murdered his wife at time t.

Can the phenomenalist construe the truth of the envisaged statement this way: 'All or most alert and enquiring beings who were at time t in the mental state described by 'I seem to see...' where the dots are filled in by an exact description of Dr Crippen's study, and who were within visual range of Dr Crippen (construed phenomenalistically) would, *if unobserved by Dr Crippen and his wife*, have seemed to see Dr Crippen murder his wife. 'The unobserved by Dr Crippen and his wife' condition is satisfied if neither Dr Crippen nor his wife would have seemed to see other humanoid bodies in their vicinity, say, because the human witnesses to the murder viewed it from a hidden location.

But suppose that Dr Crippen murdered his wife, in circumstances which were such that it was not physically *possible* for a witness to the murder to view it from a hidden location.

The answer is simply that in that case the phenomenalist needs to qualify her subjunctive conditional as follows: 'If, *contrary to fact*, it had been physically possible for witnesses to the murder to view it from a hidden location, then if they had been in that location, then. . .'

Similar considerations apply to the objection that the phenomenalist does not have the resources to construe in a plausible manner the true statement that there was a time at which there were no perceivers. If the phenomenalist wants to deny, with Berkeley, that God, like us, has visual experiences, so that the envisaged statement is *not* true, then he can construe it as follows: If, *contrary-to-fact*, it were physically possible for alert and enquiring beings to seem to see such and such a region R, of space-time, which they did not occupy, then, if they had done so, they would have failed to seem to see any perceivers at R. And so, too, for such statements as that there are at present no perceivers at the North Pole (on Mars, and so on).

8.8 My phenomenalist theory is, as it stands, incomplete. For though I have argued in effect that we are not justified in supposing that a mind-independent desk is the cause of the truth of the envisaged phenomenalist conditional, it is surely incredible that there is *no* cause of its truth. And phenomenalism, if it is unable to give a justified account of that cause, is, to that extent, defective.

But in fact Chapters 1 through 4 have put us in a position to give just such a justified account. For they warrant us in believing that God exists and is the uncreated creator of the physical universe. And, since the physical universe is arguably best construed phenomenalistically, we can know that *God* is the cause of the truth of phenomenalist conditionals.

It should be emphasized once again that we are dealing here with *theory* and not with *definition*. For the atheist surely need not be taken to be guilty of *inconsistency* when he agrees that I see my desk in my study. It is just that he does not have the right theory of what that amounts to, namely God's being disposed to cause most alert and enquiring beings, who seem to see the rest of my study, to seem to see my desk.

It is worth asking here whether theistic phenomenalism, as opposed to causal realism, represents a radical departure from common sense. Does pre-philosophical common sense rebel at the claim that it is even logically possible really to see a desk without being in a mental state which is caused by a mind-independent desk? I submit that the answer is that the pre-philosophical plain person would not know what to say if asked whether I see my desk in my study when I seem to see it, and the contemplated phenomenalist conditional is true, but God, and not a mind-independent desk, is the cause of its truth. Pre-philosophical common sense is not opposed to theistic phenomenalism. The latter is simply not within its scope.

It is, I think, clear that the pre-philosophical person *does* hold that my desk and my study *continue* to exist when no one is in my study. But, as Berkeley saw, the theistic phenomenalist agrees that my desk and my study continue to exist under those circumstances. For he holds that God is disposed, *during that period of time*, to render the consequent of the envisaged phenomenalist true when its antecedent is true.

It is also true, I think, that common sense would rebel at the idea that God is the cause of himself. Now I have argued in Chapter 1 that God exists necessarily. But that is very different from showing that God is self-caused. It is arguable that numbers exist necessarily (that is, are necessarily caused by God, a necessary being). But it is surely unlikely that this amounts to their being causes of their own existence. God's necessary existence is much better construed as his existence standing to him in the way that, say, being odd stands to the number 9. Though it is a conceptual truth that the number 9 is odd, there is surely no *causal* explanation of the fact that the number 9 is odd. The concept of the number 9, though it logically entails that the number 9 is odd, does not *cause* the number 9 to be odd.

Now, given theistic phenomenalism, God *would* be self-caused if he were essentially embodied. But in fact there is no reason to think that he is. And, indeed, in 1.7 I advanced a reason to think that he is not.

8.9   It is of note that if the arguments for God's existence, which we considered in Chapter 1, were based on claims to have made such and such *observations*, then my contention that we are justified in believing that God is the cause of the truth of the phenomenalist conditional would be subject to the following criticism: Theistic phenomenalism, which purports to be epistemically superior to causal realism with respect to the question of how I can infer a physical world from my seemings to see, must in the end admit that it is not, since it cannot give a noncircular account of the justification of observation claims. But in fact, though Berkeleyan theistic phenomenalism is subject to this criticism, my own defense of theistic phenomenalism is not, since the arguments of Chapter 1 are *a priori* ontological arguments.


8.10    There is a related objection which we need to consider here: 'The theistic phenomenalist is, in reality, no better off than the causal realist, since he is no better able to justify, on the basis of our seemings to see, *our belief in other minds* than is the causal realist to justify an inference from our seemings to see to mind-independent causes of those seemings to see. The argument from analogy for other minds is not available to the phenomenalist, since that argument requires her to be able justifiably to infer, from her observations of a repeated connection between her being in certain mental states and her engaging in certain kinds of bodily behavior, that, when she observes other humanoid bodies engaging in that kind of behavior, then they, too, are in those mental states. And prior to her using this argument, the theistic phenomenalist needs to tell us *how* she can be justified in making *those* observation claims. But since, if she subscribes to Dore's version of phenomenalism, she needs to be justified in believing that there are in fact other alert and enquiring beings in her vicinity, if she is to be justified in believing that she observes her body, it looks as if she cannot avoid circularity.'

Here the theistic phenomenalist needs to fall back on a version of the principle of credulity: 'If I seem to see humanoid bodies (including my own), then I am *prima facie* justified in believing that I do really see them.' Indeed, I think that the phenomenalist needs a *second* principle of credulity. 'When I see other humanoid bodies behaving as my body does when I am in mental state, M, I am *prima facie* justified in believing that they are in M.' For the argument from analogy is an inductive argument which is based only on my own case, and, as many philosophers have pointed out, my own case is only a very slim reed on which to base inductive generalizations and inferences.

But now why, given the former of the two principles of credulity do we *need* phenomenalism? Why should we not simply hold that, whenever we seem to see a physical object *of any sort*, there is a *prima facie* case on behalf of our really seeing it?

The answer is that the latter principle would, barring phenomenalism, justify us in inferring the existence of a myriad of physical objects *which are misdescribed by science*. For, as I pointed out in 6.12, what can be called 'the scientific desk' turns out to be very *unlike* the desk which the envisaged principle of credulity would warrant us in inferring.

But why shouldn't the nonscientific causal realist simply fall back on nonscientific realism here and maintain that it is not the job of science to give an accurate description of the *nature* of my desk, but simply to *predict* it?

One answer is that common sense does not need to be supplemented by science, when it comes to predicting the existence of my desk (it was made by carpenters), nor when it comes to predicting its existence at a later time (no one has destroyed it), nor when it comes to predicting its whereabouts at a given time (no one has removed it from my study).

But there is another answer: The nonscientific causal realist needs to give us an *explanation* of *why* science does not, and cannot, accurately describe the nature of his nonscientific desk. Why *should* that be beyond the scope of science?

The phenomenalist also needs to tell us why science cannot accurately describe the nature of my desk, *phenomenalistically construed*. But the theistic phenomenalist can easily do so. For he holds that my desk's being in my study, in reality *consists of a disposition on God's part* to bring it about that most alert and enquiring beings who are in a mental state, M, which is described by 'I seem to see . . .' where the dots are filled in by an exact description of the rest of my study, will seem to see my desk. And God's dispositions are very plainly beyond the scope of science.

It would, of course, be a good reason for rejecting phenomenalism if there were another epistemic theory which was as plausible as phenomenalism, except that it did not, in order to avoid skepticism, require the two versions of the principle of credulity which we have seen that phenomenalism requires. Skepticism-avoiding epistemic principles should not be multiplied beyond necessity. But I know of no such alternative theory.

But isn't falling back on antiskeptical epistemic principles merely an *ad hoc* refusal to accept the falsification of common sense? I think that the following argument will lend support to the envisaged principles of credulity.

Suppose that it is true that whenever I seem to see anything, I am dreaming or hallucinating. Call this proposition p. P entails that I have no observational evidence for p – that I have not, for example, veridically observed myself waking up after dreaming or falling asleep before dreaming. But such observational evidence is surely the only evidence for p that I could get. So p entails that I have no evidence for p.

Moreover, I have reason to believe that God, a supremely good being, exists, and that establishes a *prima facie* case against the claim that I never veridically see anything. So it follows from the supposition that p is true and my Chapter 1 arguments for God's existence that (a) I have no evidence *for* p and (b) I have evidence *against* it. And it follows in turn that it is irrational for me to believe p.

By the same token, my reasons for believing that God exists establish a *prima facie* case against there being at least some kinds of suffering, for example, the suffering of innocent children. But since I know that there is such suffering, *that prima facie* case has been overthrown. That is why the philosophical theist needs to show that, despite appearances, suffering is not strong evidence that God does not exist (I have tried to show this in Chapter 3). But, again, reflection shows that the *prima facie* case against God's permitting me never veridically to perceive anything cannot be even apparently overthrown.

The foregoing argument would, of course, be flagrantly circular if my putative evidence for God's existence were putative *observational* evidence. But, again, the arguments of Chapter 1 are *a priori* arguments.

I argued in 6.11 that the scientific realist, who maintains that scientific theories which predict that if we observe A-type things, we will observe B-type things, and, hence, that they predict that seeming to see A-type things is always conjoined with seeming to see B-type things, is undermined by, among other things, dreams and hallucinations.

Phenomenalism, in conjunction with the envisaged principles of credulity, does not have this problem. For what it predicts is not that, when I seem to see my desk upon seeming to see the rest of my study, at time t, I will also seem to see at t other alert and enquiring beings who behave as though they seem to see the rest of my study behaving as through they seem to see my desk, but rather that this is so *if* in fact I do seem to see other alert and enquiring beings in my study at t *and if I am not dreaming or hallucinating*.

It is of note that, if the scientific realist maintains that a given scientific theory predicts only that I will seem to see B-type things upon seeming to see A-type things, unless I am dreaming or hallucinating, then he needs to give us a different *kind* of account of how I can know at t that I am not dreaming or hallucinating. And I submit (a) that barring a principle of credulity, he cannot do so, and (b) that, as I argued in 6.12, he cannot avail himself of any principles of credulity.

But why should he not make do just with the following, very simple one: 'I am not dreaming or hallucinating.' And why should he not maintain that a given scientific theory predicts that I will seem to see B-type things upon seeming to see A-type things, *unless I am dreaming or hallucinating*? The answer is that this last claim amounts to the assertion that I will seem to see B-type things upon seeming to see A-type things *if in fact I am really seeing A-type things and B-type things*. And since we are envisaging the scientific realist offering us an *explanation* of how I can be justified in *believing* the latter, he cannot, in such a context, make such a claim.

8.11   Here the following question arises: Does my being *prima facie* justified in believing that I really see such and such a humanoid body obviate an inference, based on past experience, in conjunction with the envisaged, second version of the principle of credulity, to the conclusion that other alert and enquiring beings would seem to do so as well? How can it be the case both that I am *prima facie* justified in believing that conditional and also that I make an *inference*, based on past experience, to its truth? The point is that, given my version of phenomenalism, it may look as if my being *prima facie* justified in believing that I see a certain humanoid *body*, in a certain environment, E, is the same as my being justified in believing that God is disposed to cause most alert and enquiring beings to seem to see that body, when they seem to see E.

One answer is that most people do not have a theory of the *nature* of veridical vision, that is, they do not know what seeing a certain humanoid body consists in, and, indeed, if the overall argument of this book is sound, even most philosophers do not have a *correct* theory of the nature of veridical vision, that is, they do not know that my seeing a certain humanoid body consists in its being the case that I seem to see it, say, in my study, and that God is disposed to cause most other alert and enquiring beings who seem to see the rest of my study to seem to see that humanoid body. But now if I am justified in believing, for example, that there is a red liquid in your glass, then even though it is grape juice instead of wine, I am not justified in believing that it is grape juice, unless I have some independent evidence for that conclusion. Hence, the *prima facie* case on behalf of the envisaged philosophers and pre-philosophers really seeing another humanoid body does not obviate an inference, based on past experience, to the truth of the phenomenalist conditional. Moreover, it is open even to the phenomenalist, who *has* a correct theory of veridical vision, to maintain that the contemplated *prima facie* case *plus those past experiences which normally ground the phenomenalist inference*, make a *stronger* case for my really seeing another humanoid body than would the *prima facie* case alone.

Similar considerations hold for the application of the principle of credulity to my seeming to see, not other humanoid bodies, but, say, my desk, except that it may be that the phenomenalist should not thus extend the principle of credulity, having in mind that antiskeptical epistemic principles should be no more generous than is strictly required.

But, even if we set all this aside, it remains true that theistic phenomenalism, plus the contemplated principles of credulity, gives us a theory of veridical vision which is epistemically superior to scientific causal realism, since the latter theory, but not the former one, fails to account adequately for the empirical basis of science, non-realistically construed. Moreover, as I have argued, *non*scientific causal realism is really no better off than the scientific variety.

But *does* the former theory really tell us *why* scientific theories, nonrealistically construed, predict observations, phenomenalistically construed? Suppose that this question is taken as an abbreviation of a large number of more specific questions, such as 'Why does quark theory predict observations which consist of our really seeing precisely what we seem to see?' The answer is that the scientific theorist-cum-philosopher can tell us, or that the philosopher-cum-scientific theorist can tell us, but that the answer is beyond the competence of the philosopher *qua* philosopher, and, perhaps, of the scientist *qua* scientist. But the philosopher *qua* philosopher can say this much: 'Relatively simple scientific theories predict our observations because that is what they were *designed* to do. And scientists have learned, by trial and error, over roughly the last five centuries, how to succeed in designing such theories.'

But how, exactly, does my version of phenomenalism avoid the regress which I have imputed to the scientific realist? The reader will recall that I imagined him advancing the following argument: 'Scientific theories, realistically construed, predict "seemings-to-see" which, if they occur, validate those theories.' My reply was that the envisaged scientific theories must be based in part on observations, and, that, since observations demonstrably involve seemings-to-see, the causal realist, who argues that *those* seemings-to-see are also predicted by observation-based scientific theories, is started on an unacceptable regress.

The phenomenalist, on the other hand, can get us to 'the external world' (to objects like my desk), without falling back on an observation-based scientific theory, by the simple expedient of maintaining that I am warranted in believing that my desk exists in my study because (a) I am warranted in believing that other alert and enquiring beings who seemed to see my study would seem to see my desk and (b) that *that* belief is, roughly speaking, all that my belief that my desk is in my study should amount to. (I say 'roughly speaking,' since, as we have seen, phenomenalism requires theism.)

8.12  Theistic phenomenalism, as opposed to scientific realism, can be supported by the following consideration. We know from Chapters 1 to 4 that God is the cause of the physical universe. But, given scientific realism, it is impossible to understand just what his causation consists in. He cannot have been a *temporally first* cause, since space-time began with the big bang. But it is surely incredible both that scientific realism is true and that it does not provide us with a perfectly adequate explanation of things *from moment to moment*. In short if scientific realism is true, then, regarding God's causation, not only do 'we have no *need* of that hypothesis', the claim that God is the cause of the physical universe is clearly false. But in fact it is demonstrably true. It follows, once again, that scientific realism is false.

The reader may have asked herself how God can be the uncreated creator of the physical universe and everything in it, if quantum theory is true, that is, if there are uncaused physical events. A simple answer is now available: quantum theory, though highly predictive and relatively simple, is not true of mind-independent events. (Had Einstein not been a scientific realist, he might well have had less trouble with quantum theory.)

8.13  Let us return to the drug of 7.5, which putatively causes the existence of my desk, since it putatively causes the relevant phenomenalist conditional to be true. Since God is demonstrably the ultimate cause of the truth of that conditional, we can look at the drug as, in the envisaged circumstances, *revealing* to us that the desk exists in my study. The claim that the drug causes us to recognize that that conditional is true is, barring some ultimate cause of its being true other than the drug itself, simply an uneconomical way of saying that the drug causes the phenomenalist conditional to be true *simpliciter*, and hence, causes the existence of my desk *simpliciter*. And that is, indeed, strongly counter-intuitive. But we now know that God, and not the drug, would be the ultimate cause of the truth of the envisaged conditional. And so we can treat the drug as being analogous to a powerful microscope. Just as the microscope does not cause what we see through it to exist, even though God would not be disposed to cause us to see what we see through it, if we did not use the microscope, so too, it is open to the phenomenalist to construe the envisaged drug, not as causing the existence of my desk, but as enabling us to see it, where seeing it is construed in terms of theistic phenomenalism.

But is it not *possible*, at least, that the drug alone is the cause of the truth of the relevant phenomenalist conditional, that is, isn't it possible that God is *not* its ultimate cause? If so, then I am committed to the implausible thesis that it is at least possible for a drug to cause my desk to exist, even though God does not.

One answer to the envisaged question is that God demonstrably exists necessarily and is necessarily the uncreated creator of the drug, so that it is not in fact possible for him not to be the ultimate cause of the existence of my desk. And a related answer is that, since the truth of the envisaged phenomenalist conditional is sufficient for the existence of my desk, it is *eo ipso* sufficient for God, who is necessarily the uncreated creator *of desks*, to be the ultimate cause of the truth of that conditional. And that in turn is sufficient for the drug's *revealing* the existence of the desk, rather than *causing* it.

8.14  Finally, I have formulated the phenomenalist subjunctive conditional in terms of what I have called 'The environment condition,' that is, in terms of the mental state which is picked out by 'I seem to see. . .' where the dots are filled in by an exact description of the physical environment of the object which I seem to see. And it may be objected that, in so doing, I have begged the question against the perceptual skeptic by presupposing that in fact the objects which I seem to see are in fact frequently in such and such a physical environment. But I am addressing myself to the perceptual skeptic only to the extent that he claims to have plausible arguments for his position. And, I submit that, given theistic phenomenalism, he has none.

But can I understand what is meant by 'I seem to see such and such a physical environment', unless I understand what it would be like really to see one? The answer certainly appears to be 'No'. But that surely does not entail that I cannot understand what is meant by 'I seem to see physical environment E' unless I know that I, or others, really have seen E.

# Appendix I

There is more to be said about science. Imagine that a skeptic raises the following objection: 'Dore maintains that scientific theories are acceptable because (and only because) they are predictively fruitful. But, in fact, if Dore is right they are not. For they entail such claims as that Dore's desk is mainly empty space. And if Dore's version of phenomenalism were true, then *ipso facto* they would entail that all or most alert and enquiring beings who seemed to see the rest of Dore's study, *would seem to see a desk which consists mainly of empty space*. But that is, as we know, false. Hence, Dore cannot after all sustain a non-realist, instrumentalist justification of science.'

But in fact the claim that my desk is mainly empty space entails that, when we see my desk, we will seem to see mainly empty space, only in conjunction with some scientific theory of vision. And since we know that we do not seem to see mainly empty space when we seem to see my desk, we can be sure that any such theory of vision is false.

But now the nonskeptical realist may argue as follows: 'Scientific theories of vision can take the place of the principle of credulity, in supporting scientific realism. Scientific theories can, indeed predict our seemings-to-see, in conjunction with scientific theories of vision. Moreover, there is no reason to believe that there are some scientific theories which cannot do this. Hence, all scientific theories can be confirmed (or, of course, disconfirmed) by the consideration that they are accurate (or inaccurate) predicters of our seemings-to-see.'

But I have, in effect, answered this objection in 6.11. First, even given sound scientific theories of vision, they do not contribute to making accurate predictions of the seeming perceptions which are involved in many dreams and hallucinations. And, second, scientific theories of vision must, like all scientific theories, be backed by observations. And the claim that these observations are, at least in part, backed by scientific theories of vision starts us on an unacceptable regress.

Here the skeptic may press his case as follows: 'Regardless of whether the scientific theories, which entail that Dore's desk is mainly empty space, are inaccurate (false) predicters of our seemings to see, it remains true that they are false. For they entail the false statement that Dore's desk is mainly empty space.'

The answer is that, since those higher level theories are essentially predictions, it is likely that 'Dore's desk is mainly empty space' is not a nonpredictive description of the nature of Dore's desk, but a prediction. But what, precisely, does it predict? The answer is that the envisaged statement predicts, in conjunction with other, more general scientific theories, what we would seem to see, were we to view my desk under a powerful microscope.

It is of note that the concept of a powerful microscope allows the phenomenalist to grant that it may be that electrons and the like really exist, in the sense that it is physically possible for there to be microscopes which are sufficiently powerful so that we would seem to see electrons, and so on, were we to use them. Indeed, as I pointed out in 6.13, it is at present possible to view heavy molecules under an electron microscope. (It should be emphasized, however, that the fact that molecular theory predicts that we will see heavy molecules under an electron microscope is not a good reason for accepting a nonphenomenalistic, realist interpretation of molecular theory. For molecular theory does not enable us to verify the claim that we are veridically seeing – as opposed to just seeming to see – heavy molecules. That inference is a prescientific inference, which is justified only if my version of phenomenalism is true.)

Is it also at present possible to view electrons in a cloud chamber? Or do we observe only electron tracks? The answer is that the phenomenalist, *qua* phenomenalist, need not answer this question one way or the other. The important point is that, though 'Dore's desk is mainly empty space' is not a true, nonpredictive description of Dore's desk, it is a true predicter of what we do or would, under certain circumstances, seem to see.

Finally, we now have the resources to deal with this objection: 'Dore is in effect rejecting the claim that his desk, scientifically construed, is a cause of his seeming to see his desk. But then consistency obliges him to reject the other links in the causal chain, which science posits, that is, Dore's desk reflecting light waves, which stimulate his retinas, which activate his optic nerves, which give use to certain activities in his visual cortex. And surely that entails that the various sciences of vision are, after all, false. For there is clearly no adequate pragmatic-instrumentalist interpretation of optics, neurophysiology, and the other sciences of vision, all of which are essentially causal theories of vision.'

The answer is that we can give such an interpretation, since we can give a phenomenalist construal of, say, the claim that certain processes, P, in my visual cortex give rise to my seeming to see my desk on a given occasion O, namely, the following: 'It is causally necessary and sufficient for my seeming to see my desk on occasion O that all or most alert and enquiring beings who detect P (via a sophisticated brain machine) would detect that I seem to see my desk.' The conditional can then be construed phenomenalistically by substituting 'seem to see. . .' for 'detect' Moreover, the phenomenalist can leave it an open question as to whether P's occurring is just P's-being-thus-detected (that is, 'P-traces') or whether it is possible to observe P – just as he can leave it an open question as to whether it is possible to observe electrons.

The claim that my desk, scientifically construed, causes me to seem to see it on a given occasion O can then be pragmatically-instrumentally interpreted via the following phenomenalist construal: 'It is causally necessary and sufficient for my seeming to see my desk or occasion O that all or most alert and enquiring beings who detected my desk, scientifically construed, would detect its reflecting light waves, which, and so on', where detecting those things is interpreted in terms of seemings-to-see.

But doesn't the claim that brain processes – which are themselves construed in terms of seemings-to-see – cause seemings-to-see start us on an unacceptable regress? Isn't it true that if brain processes are, in part, reducible to seemings-to-see, then not all seemings-to-see can be caused by brain processes? In particular, not all the seemings-to-see to which brain processes are, in part, reducible can be so caused. That is to say, if each such set of seemings-to-see is caused by a brain process, which itself is, in part, reducible to seemings-to-see, which are in turn caused by brain processes, then we are started on a vicious regress.

The conclusion that I draw here is that we can know *a priori* that the regress does in fact terminate at some point at which God is the direct (sole) cause of the seemings-to-see, in terms of which those brain processes which cause the next level of seemings-to-see can be construed, though it is an empirical question as to where the regress breaks off. There is an analogy. Consider scientific explanations of the form '$E_1$ is an explainer of X; and $E_2$ is an explainer of $E_1$; and $E_3$

is an explainer of $E_2$; and so on'. No matter what theory of the nature of scientific explanation we may subscribe to, we can know *a priori* that the envisaged regress breaks off at some point, though it is an empirical question as to where it ends.

# Appendix II

Shall we hold that God is, in fact, the direct, regress-ending cause of some actual body-cum-brain seemings-to-see or shall we hold instead just that God is *disposed* to be such a direct cause at some point in the envisaged regress which has not yet been reached?

The considerations set out in Chapter 4 should incline us to accept the former thesis (see especially 4.8). Since the seemings-to-see which are directly caused by God are *a fortiori* not causally linked to physical brain processes, the fact that the latter are perishable does not entail that the former are perishable.

More generally, my *body* is causally necessary and sufficient for some of my seemings-to-see, and my body is construable in terms of body seemings-to-see. But this regress must have an end. And if it ends in my body, then phenomenalism is after all false. Hence, the fact that my body is perishable does not entail that my body seemings-to-see are perishable.

At this stage, they will not exist *in the physical* universe, since a necessary condition of existing in the physical universe is *being causally connected to* other physical things, and body-cum-brain seemings-to-see are causally connected to other physical things, only if they are (as *ex hypothesi* they are *not* at this stage) causally connected to my body.

But now if it is plausible that God is the direct cause of *brain* and *body* seemings-to-see, then it is plausible that he directly causes *other kinds* of seemings-to-see at the stage where *no* seemings-to-see are causally connected to bodies-cum-brains. But, again, *none* of these seemings-to-see are part of the physical universe, since *ex hypothesis* they have no causal connections with physical things. Hence, we can exist in a world which is phenomenologically very much like the present one, even though our physical bodies-cum-brains have perished, that is, even though body-cum-brain seemings-to-see are no longer part of the physical universe, because no longer causally linked to bodies-cum-brains.

# Appendix III

Richard Swinburne has recently advanced an argument, based on scientific cosmology, for the existence of God. And it may well be thought that if God's existence really is a sound scientific hypothesis, then we need only wait on the progress of science to discover precisely how God grounds the physical universe.

In *Physical Cosmology and Philosophy*,[1] Swinburne sets out what he calls 'the argument from fine tuning.' The essence of his argument can be found on p. 164:

> [T]he range of [fundamental constants] allowing life is probably very small indeed . . . the best policy for assessing the worth of the argument from fine-tuning [is] initially to suppose background knowledge (k), that the Universe began from an initial singularity and that laws have the form of our four-force laws, and then consider the force of the further evidence (e) that the initial condition and constants of laws had just those values which allowed [intelligent] life to evolve. *A priori* that is very unlikely but much to be expected if there is a God (h). Hence, since $P(e/h.k) \gg P(e/k)$, $P(h/e.k) \gg P(h/k)$.

The formula can be translated as follows: 'Since the probability of intelligent life, given God and the envisaged background knowledge, is statistically significantly greater than the probability of intelligent life, given just that background knowledge, the probability of God, given intelligent life and that background knowledge, is significantly greater than the probability of intelligent life, given just that background knowledge.' For simplicity, I shall sum this up by saying that since the probability of (e), given (h) and (k), is significantly greater than probability of (e), given just (k), (e) predicts (and so confirms) (h). I shall not try to formulate a phenomenalist version of Swinburne's argument. The question of whether an adequate phenomenalist account of the argument is available, or whether it is essentially a piece of scientific realism, need not trouble us, since the argument is demonstrably flawed.

Swinburne's argument that (h) predicts (e) is roughly that since intelligent life is the most valuable thing in the physical universe and since God, if he exists, is perfectly good, he would want to be the author of embodied intelligent life therein.[2] Now I think that, barring arguments for God's existence other than the present one, the hypothesis that there is an immensely powerful demon who wants there to be intelligent life, since intelligent beings suffer more than nonintelligent beings, is as successful a predictor of intelligent life in the physical universe as is (h). But let us set that consideration aside. Still, problems remain.

As we have seen, Swinburne maintains that the fundamental constants which allowed intelligent life to evolve are 'a priori . . . very unlikely, but much to be expected if there is a God',[3] So we need to ask what theory of probability (what interpretation of the probability calculus) Swinburne has in mind here. Since he says that those constants are *a priori* very unlikely, it is reasonable to suppose that he is a Laplacean equi-possibility theorist, who holds that possible universes with fundamental constants which give rise to intelligent life are very improbable, since they are enormously outnumbered by equi-possible universes which do not contain those constants. But, in fact, equi-possibility theory is mistaken: we cannot estimate equi-possibilities in an empirical vacuum. Consider the following pseudo-argument: 'There is either no extraterrestrial intelligent being, or there is one such being or there are two such beings or three or four or five or, and so on. Hence it is enormously improbable that there is no such being.' I do not mean to deny here that there is in fact extraterrestrial intelligent life. I intend only to point out that equi-possibility theory will not thus enable us to establish that there is; and the reason is evidently that we are not warranted in affirming *a priori* that the envisaged alternatives are all equi-possible.

There is another related criticism of Swinburne. Suppose that equi-possibility theory were, in fact, acceptable. Then the existence of exactly *one* good intelligent cause, call him $B_1$, of *other* intelligent beings would be enormously improbable. And there is no apparent reason why *another* such being, call her $B_2$, would not predict the existence of $B_1$, since $B_2$, a good being, would want to bring $B_1$, a good intelligent being, into existence.

But now we are started on an unacceptable regress. And if Swinburne tries to avoid it by falling back on *simplicity*, then the reply is that it is still simpler not even to affirm the existence of $B_1$.

I characterize $B_1$ and $B_2$ as 'good' rather than 'perfectly good,' since, as we saw in 1.4, only (exactly) one perfectly good being is possible. So the regress to which Swinburne is committed is not a regress involving supremely perfect beings, that is, Swinburne is not committed to the existence of more than one God. But he *is* committed to a regress of (good) intelligent gods, each one of which is the creator of another such god. And this should surely give him pause.

# Appendix IV

My defense of phenomenalism can be buttressed by the following considerations: It is very clear to some philosophers that (a) there are such things as qualia, for example, visual experiences of red objects, the taste of a pineapple, the smell of burning leaves, and so on, and (b) that it is false that these are identical with brain processes. Let us concentrate on visual experiences of color for a time. There is a simple argument for (b): a person who has been blind from birth cannot know what a visual experience of a red object is like, no matter how sophisticated she may be about the neurophysiology of vision. With regard to the denial of (a) (for example, of visual experiences), I submit that I have shown in Chapter 8 that this is in effect a denial of the claim that we ever see anything. And I take that to be unacceptable.

Regarding (b), Daniel Dennett has recently denied that the envisaged argument on its behalf is sound. Dennett claims in effect that if a person who has been blind from birth could know as much as can possibly be known about the sciences of vision, then she *would* know what it is like to have a visual experience of a red object.[1] One problem with this latter claim is that Dennett needs to tell us precisely *why* a blind-from-birth neurophysiologist doesn't *already* have enough scientific sophistication to know what it is like to have such a visual experience. And, anyway, Dennett's overall argument looks to be flatly counter-intuitive. Let me risk appearing melodramatic here: Is Dennett really prepared to say that a sophisticated sex researcher who has never been sexually sensitive can, or could, know what it is like to have an orgasm?

In view of the above, I submit (a) that there are such things as qualia (that is, that there is such a thing as consciousness) and (b) that, unless we are willing to accept radical mind-body dualism, we should prefer the claim (1) that brain processes, like other physical processes, are best construed as dispositions on God's part to produce brain-process-qualia in all or most alert and inquiring sentient beings who satisfy certain environmental conditions (which are themselves construable in terms of theistic phenomenalism) to the claim (2) that qualia are nothing but brain processes. (If we attempt to embrace *both* (1) and (2), then another unacceptable regress looms: qualia are identical with brain processes which are best construed in terms of qualia, and so on.)

Finally, why *shouldn't* we accept nonphenomenalistic dualism? It may be said here that even the phenomenalist must accept a *variety* of dualism, in view of the fact that brain states, whether phenomenalistically construed or not, are causally connected with states of consciousness.

There are a number of replies: (a) Phenomenalist dualism is much more innocuous than standard dualism, inasmuch as qualia and brain processes do not belong to different ontological kinds (since the latter are best construed in terms of the former). (b) The claim that it is causally impossible for there to be qualia in the absence of brain processes leads, given phenomenalism, to an unacceptable regress. So the phenomenalist is committed to a rejection of epiphenomenalism. (c) And *qua* theist, he is committed to a rejection of interactionism. My mental states do not cause changes in my body. The latter are best construed as dispositions on God's part to cause certain seemings-to-see, given certain other seemings-to-see (that is, given that a certain environment condition is satisfied). My decisions *do* bring it about that God has that disposition. But no theist who believes (as most theists do) in divine-human interaction (for example, in petitionary prayer) will be distressed by that conclusion.

# Notes

## 1 THE CONCEPT OF SUPREME PERFECTION

1. By 'the Gaunilo-strategy' I mean to refer to a parody of the original ontological argument, formulated by St Anselm in the late eleventh Century, which was produced by a fellow monastic, Gaunilo, and which keeps reemerging in different forms vis-à-vis different versions of the ontological argument.

## 2 THE ARGUMENT FROM SUFFERING I

1. Alvin Plantinga, *God and Other Minds* (Ithaca: Cornell University Press, 1967) Chapters 5 and 6, pp. 164–95. His later writings on the subject in, for example, *The Nature of Necessity* (Oxford, Clarendon Press: 1974) pp. 164–95, give us no reason to think that he wishes to repudiate this version, only to elaborate on it. Plantinga distinguishes between what he calls the 'logical' and the 'probabilistic' forms of the problem of suffering. I shall be exploring the question of whether the free will defense constitutes a sound solution of both problems. This will not result in an injustice to Plantinga, since, so far as I can see, he maintains in effect that it does. (See footnote 6.)
2. By 'logically (im)possible' I shall mean '(not) broadly logically possible' in Plantinga's sense of 'broadly logically possible'. Alvin Plantinga, *The Nature of Necessity*, *ibid.*, Chapter 1.
3. *Ibid.*, pp. 186–9.
4. J. L. Mackie, *The Miracle of Theism* (New York: Oxford University Press, 1982) p. 174.
5. R. M. Adams claims in effect that conditionals of the following kind have no truth value and *a fortiori* are such that even God could not know that they are true: 'If, contrary to fact, Jones had been going to perform a given action on a given occasion, and this action would not have been causally determined (and, hence, unfree), then . . .' (R. M. Adams, 'Middle Knowledge and the Problem of Evil', *American Philosophical Quarterly*, 14 (April 1977).) My intuitions about this matter differ from Adams's, but if in fact Adams is right, then he has presented us with an alternative explanation of why God is not disposed to intervene: He cannot know whether or not such intervention is necessary; and if he tried to play it safe, he would abolish free will.

6.  Plantinga advances a similar argument in 'The Probabilistic Argument from Evil', *Philosophical Studies* 35 (1979), p. 46. He appears to believe that his rebuttal does not, strictly speaking, require that argument. If, in fact, that is his position, then I disagree.
7.  Alvin Plantinga, 'Reason and Belief in God', in Plantinga and Wotterstorff (ed.), *Faith and Rationality* (Notre Dame: University of Notre Dame Press, 1983) pp. 16–93.
8.  See, for example, Gilbert Harman, 'Positive Versus Negative Undermining in Belief Revision', *Nôus* 18 (1984), pp. 39–49.
9.  Harry G. Frankfurt, 'Alternate Possibilities and Moral Responsibility', *Journal of Philosophy* (December, 1969) pp. 828–39.

## 3  THE ARGUMENT FROM SUFFERING II

1.  Thomas Morris, *The Logic of God Incarnate* (Ithaca, NY: Cornell University Press, 1986).

## 4  HOW GOD GROUNDS MORALITY I

1.  R. M. Hare, *Moral Thinking* (New York: Oxford University Press, 1981) pp. 60–1.

## 6  HOW TO APPLY THE IDEAL OBSERVER THEORY

1.  Gilbert Harman, *The Nature of Morality* (New York: Oxford University Press, 1977) p. 156.
2.  Michael Tooley, 'A Defense of Abortion and Infanticide', in Joel Feinberg (ed.), 1st edn (Belmont, California: Wadsworth, 1973) pp. 51–91, and 'A Defense of Abortion and Infanticide', in Feinberg, *The Problem of Abortion*, 2nd edn (1984) pp. 120–34. I shall consider only the first of these two articles, since I think that the arguments in the first one are more persuasive than those in the second.
3.  Philippa Foot, *Virtues and Vices* and *Other Essays in Moral Philosophy* (Berkeley: University of California Press, 1978) p. 29.

## 7  CAUSAL REALISM AND THE EGOCENTRIC PREDICAMENT

1.  Gilbert Ryle, 'Sensation,' in H. D. Lewis (ed.), *Contemporary British Philosophy*, 3rd edn (New York: Macmillan, 1956), p. 435.
2.  G. J. Warnock, *Berkeley* (Harmondsworth: Penguin, 1953), p. 186.
3.  Unless, of course, they are placed in quotation marks and used to refer to word types or tokens.
4.  It might be thought that the speaker's being sure that it will rain falsifies what he says, and that the same is true of his being certain that it will not rain. But this is a mistake, since 'Maybe it will rain

today' does not, strictly speaking, *assert* that the speaker is uncertain about whether it will rain. The speaker is, of course, being *misleading* if he is convinced that it will rain or convinced that it will not.

5.  D. M. Armstrong, *A Materialist Theory of Mind* (London: Routledge & Kegan Paul, 1968) p. 222.
6.  Ibid., p. 223.
7.  Ibid.
8.  Ibid.
9.  Ibid., p. 224
10. In case it is objected here that quantum theory holds that there is no empty space in my desk, since 'clouds' of electrons permeate it, one answer is that in appearing to be solid, my desk appears not to be composed in part of nonsolid clouds. And, anyway, quantum theory has the Rutherford model of the atom, which is composed mainly of empty space, as part of its epistemic background, and so quantum theory cannot have been based in part on an application of the principle of credulity.
11. Saul Kripke, *Wittgenstein on Rules and Private Language* (Cambridge: Harvard University Press, 1982) p. 20.

## APPENDIX III

1.  John Leslie (ed.), *Physical Cosmology and Philosophy* (New York: Macmillan Publishing Company, 1990).
2.  Ibid., pp. 155–6.
3.  Ibid., p. 164.

## APPENDIX IV

1.  Daniel Dennett, *Consciousness Explained* (Boston: Little, Brown and Company, 1991) pp. 398–400.

# Index

## DATE DUE

| | | | |
|---|---|---|---|
| | | | |
| | | | |
| | | | |
| | | | |
| | | | |
| | | | |
| | | | |
| | | | |
| | | | |
| | | | |
| | | | |
| | | | |
| | | | |
| | | | |
| | | | |
| | | | |
| | | | |
| | | | Printed in USA |

HIGHSMITH #45230